The Mother, the Son, and the Socialite

The True Story of a Mother-Son Crime Spree

ADRIAN HAVILL

St. Martin's Paperbacks

THE MOTHER, THE SON, AND THE SOCIALITE

Copyright © 1999 by Adrian Havill.

Cover photographs courtesy AP/Wide World Photos.

ISBN: 0-312-97069-2

Printed in the United States of America

St. Martin's Paperbacks edition/April 1999

10   9   8   7   6   5   4   3

Dear Reader:

The book you are about to read is the latest bestseller from St. Martin's True Crime Library, the imprint *The New York Times* calls "the leader in true crime!" Each month, we offer you a fascinating account of the latest, most sensational crime that has captured the national attention. St. Martin's is the publisher of perennial bestselling true crime author Jack Olsen (SON and DOC) whose SALT OF THE EARTH is the true story of how one woman fought and triumphed over life-shattering violence; Joseph Wambaugh called it "powerful and absorbing." DEATH OF A LITTLE PRINCESS recounts the investigation into the horrifying murder of child beauty queen JonBenét Ramsey; the author is Carlton Smith. Fannie Weinstein and Melinda Wilson tell the story of a beautiful honors student who was lured into the dark world of sex for hire in THE COED CALL GIRL MURDER.

St. Martin's True Crime Library gives you the stories *behind* the headlines. Our authors take you right to the scene of the crime and into the minds of the most notorious murderers to show you what really makes them tick. St. Martin's True Crime Library paperbacks are better than the most terrifying thriller, because it's all true! The next time you want a crackling good read, make sure it's got the St. Martin's True Crime Library logo on the spine—you'll be up all night!

Charles E. Spicer, Jr.
Senior Editor, St. Martin's True Crime Library

Like Mother, Like Son.
A Dangerous Team Scams Its Way Across the Country:

September, 1996, Bahamas. Sayed Bilal Ahmed, 53, a banker with whom the Kimeses had dinner, suddenly vanishes.

January, 1998, Las Vegas. Sante Kimes is a suspect in the fire of her home—a possible arson attempt to collect insurance money.

March, 1998, Los Angeles. Fifty-three-year-old businessman David Kazdin is found dead in a trash bin, shot with a .22-caliber bullet. The Kimeses, with whom Kazdin had business dealings, are major suspects in his death.

April, 1998, Salt Lake City. Mother and son purchase a Lincoln Town Car with a $14,000 rubber check.

July, 1998, New York City. Irene Silverman vanishes, as the Kimeses are apprehended and are primary suspects in her disappearance.

Praise for *The Mother, the Son, and the Socialite:*

"Crime journalism at its best! Well-written, carefully researched, and as timely as the headlines that captured attention from coast-to-coast."
—Jack Olsen, bestselling author of HASTENED TO THE GRAVE and SALT OF THE EARTH

"An instant true-crime classic! Gritty and riveting!"
—Larry Celona,
Police Reporter, *New York Post*

This Book Is For:
Amanda and Rich,
David and Mami.

Contents

Introduction

"To grift" is defined by *Webster's* as a method for obtaining money falsely through swindles, frauds, dishonesty, or rigged gambling. Certainly Sante Kimes (rhymes with crimes) has spent much of her adult life as a confidence artist or grifter, as well as being a convicted thief and keeper of slaves. In recent years, her son Kenny appears to have joined her, replacing her late husband in what had become a family enterprise.

Grifters are the Einsteins of crime. They use smarts, wit, and cunning to separate their victims from property and money. If one can admire a criminal, then the grifters have become our folk heroes, immortalized by journalists and film makers, who have portrayed them as lovable scam artists who usually prey on the rich and famous. We love to read about their intricate pull-the-wool-over-the-eyes deeds that have been given exotic names like the "pigeon drop" or the "scoop and squat."

Con artists often count on the greed of their prey to temporarily blind them. It is at that precise point at which they press their advantage and make the score.

Is there a more classic scam than the infamous Ponzi scheme, still practiced today? Named for Charles Ponzi, its inventor, the plan is simple. Convince avaricious speculators that you will double their money in a couple of months. You then pay off the first plungers as promised, have them find a dozen or more friends, and quickly take the remaining victims' money and disappear.

A woman by the name of Cassie Chadwick once traveled the country persuading bankers she was the daughter of industrialist Andrew Carnegie. She raked in more than a million dollars. In recent years, a variation of this scam has appeared. Celebrity lookalikes roam the country, taking advantage of hotel, restaurant, and limousine service managers' belief that they are A-list movie stars. After allowing themselves to be wined and dined for days, they disappear, often leaving the hotel management so embarrassed that no charges are filed.

In fact, that seems to have once been a favorite ploy of the central character of this tale. Sante Kimes once looked so much like the actress Elizabeth Taylor that she would often sign autographs in Taylor's name when mistaken for her. Like Ms. Chadwick, she also used the resemblance to someone famous to demand special services from hospitality purveyors.

"I never cheated an honest man, only rascals," said the notorious grifter Yellow Kid Weil, who lived off con games for thirty-five years. He despised his quarry.

"They may have been respectable, but they were never any good. They wanted something for nothing. And I gave them nothing for something."

Then there are the "con Juans," grifters who romance wealthy women out of their assets through sequential marriages or serial cohabitation. Their victims rarely complain, so deep is the chagrin they feel after the relationship is over and their money has all but disappeared.

Our police often play deceit games of their own. They call it a *sting*. Who among us hasn't seen these hidden camera tapes on television? The thieves are lured to a phony pawn shop operated by lawmen who pay higher prices to the bad guys than the fence next door. We rejoice in the cops' con as the camera zooms in on the hapless crook as he is arrested walking out the door. And who doesn't know the trick of telephoning fugitives holed up in a high-rise hideout? The detective impersonates a pitchman, informing them they've just won a lottery, sweepstakes, or some such ploy, then slaps on the handcuffs as they eagerly appear at the law agency's door seeking their grand prize.

America is in many ways a nation of con men and women. It starts at the bottom, with three-card monte dealers and shell game sleight-of-hand artists in the darker corners off New York's Broadway. On a higher level, there are the more sophisticated sellers of gold bullion that the mark later finds is plated, or the slick society grifters who count on avarice in order to slip rich swells black-market Old Masters that have been cleverly forged. Then there are the penny stock hustlers and the imaginary charity marketeers who make their pitches by phone from windowless boiler rooms, beguiling the gullible into mailing them checks.

The perpetrators of these acts get away with their schemes more often than not. Their more obvious criminal brethren who crudely hit, snatch, or grab, then run, are considered to be of a lower outlaw class.

Fugitive grifters are not a high priority for the enforcers of U.S. law. The swindler has usually moved on to another city in another state by the time a report is received. The victims often delay notifying the police, so embarrassed or disbelieving are they of their misfortune. Grifters are hard to trace, usually altering their Social Security numbers by one or two digits every chance they get, as well as constantly changing their names or assuming the identity of a deceased person. Knowing the difficulty of finding these people and believing that apprehending violent criminals is more important, police departments have unwritten policies that allow the grifter to roam the nation with little fear of pursuit.

On the other hand, a perpetrator of multiple murders gets far and away the highest attention afforded any suspect by every law-enforcement agency in the land. Homicide is a headline grabber. Violent deaths—television's credo is "If it bleeds, it leads"—are the first items on your local evening news.

There are three types of multiple murderers—mass murderers, serial murderers, and spree murderers.

A mass murderer kills all his victims within a short time span. He needs three or more deaths to qualify for this dubious honor. Former altar boy and Eagle Scout Charles

Whitman, who, on August 1, 1966, shot and killed twelve people from the observation tower of the University of Texas in Austin, while wounding thirty, after having earlier murdered two relatives, is one such bloody example. Richard Speck, who killed eight nursing students within hours inside a Chicago townhouse the same year, is another. Mass murderers are often considered mentally deranged, with good reason.

Serial murderers, while also often mentally impaired, are much harder to apprehend. The serial killer plans the demise of his quarry meticulously for months, usually killing for sexual gratification. A serial killer fantasizes about the act both before and after the deed. He stalks his prey (he is virtually always a male) and, after dispatching the victim, either takes several personal items so he can relive the gruesome episode or returns to the scene of the crime again and again so that he can repeat and fantasize about the experience of the act.

Many serial killers, such as John Wayne Gacy and Jeffrey Dahmer, like to keep their dead close by. Real close by. Gacy buried dozens of his young victims under the floorboards of his suburban Chicago home. Dahmer kept the heads and other body parts of his prey in the refrigerator of his Milwaukee apartment. The police discovered that he had drilled into the brains of those chilled deceased. Battery acid had been poured into those holes. It was Dahmer's goal to create a "sex zombie." His deepest desire was to create a sex partner who was still alive but brain dead.

Spree killings are the hardest multiple murders to solve. They fall under what the FBI terms a *disorganized* crime. The murders are often commited several different ways. There is no pattern for the police to follow and, unlike the serial killer, who is territorial, the spree killer can often strike anywhere without long premeditation. Andrew Cunanan, who murdered the fashion designer Gianni Versace and several other acquaintances, each in a different state, was termed a serial murderer in the nation's press, but an FBI profiler would classify him as a spree killer.

Noted criminologist Robert K. Ressler once told an FBI training class that America is "baseball, mom, apple pie, and serial killers.'' According to Ressler, seventy-five percent of the world's multiple murderers are Americans. The U.S. has the distinction of global leadership in these categories, and is far ahead of all other industrialized countries combined in every mass, serial, and spree murder count that's taken. Call it a cartel if you like, but America dominates this bloody business much as South Africa does diamonds.

Grifting is not supposed to go with murder like hamburgers go with fries. Especially not several murders. Now, for the first time in the U.S., the two may have converged. Our own venerable *Time* magazine has written that ''the Kimeses may be the biggest mother-and-son crime team since Ma Barker and her boys.'' That's fascinating, since, as the readers of this book will learn, the Kimeses are directly linked to the Barker gang of the 1920s.

Have Sante Kimes and her son Kenny carved out a new niche in this shameful section of American behavior? Certainly never before has a mother-and-son team been suspected of so many different murders.

Probably, both of them could have stayed under the legal radar for many more years if they had stuck to a life of simple scams and cons. But, to get the big score, you often have to take big risks, even if the risk may involve murder.

On July 5, 1998, a deadly gamble, which may have been taken by Sante and Kenny Kimes, might soon be shown to be their undoing.

Adrian Havill
Reston, Virginia
January 1999

PART ONE

The people they deal with keep coming up
dead . . . This is the kind of thing that makes
you want to lock your door at night.

Jim Blackner
Cedar City, Utah

Prologue

The carved stone face had been placed just above the door of the fashionable, five-story, gray limestone mansion at 20 East 65th Street. The builder had installed it there because a legend said the face was a symbol of good luck and would ward off evil. Its godlike countenance had been sculpted around the turn of the century, most likely by Karl Bitter, the sculptor of the majestic, six-level fountain in front of New York's fabled Plaza Hotel and a disciple of famed architect Stanford White. Wings sprang from the temples of its head, ordaining it with the mythical ability to fly away into the darkness at the stroke of midnight in search of bacchanalian revelry.

For nearly a century, according to legend, the god face had always faithfully returned each dawn to resume guarding the entrance of the grand city house and the occupants within. The fierce open mouth appeared to make it a gargoyle—a functioning waterspout. Since no water had ever spewed from the lips of the statue it was more correctly termed by art mavens a *grotesque*. These great stone carvings were a centuries-old tradition on many of the grander buildings in New York City.

Only this morning, the great carved face was failing to do its job.

It was nearly noon on July 5, 1998, and, on this Sunday after the loudest, most celebratory of all American holidays, the city slept even later than usual. The shops and restaurants were still mostly closed. Those stores that would do business that day had scheduled their openings to begin an hour later, at one in the afternoon. To be sure, this fashionable side street, the first block off Central Park, was not completely deserted. A dog-walker passed. A runner jogged by. A young single woman, her career ambition so defined by her clothing and hairstyle that she might have worn a uniform, strolled home from a Saturday night stay at her lover's apartment. Like most Manhattanites, their curiosity was kept purposely in check. Any thoughts they had stayed within them.

And a man and woman moving a few possessions out of a residential building on a Sunday morning was not an event one would stay to watch or even notice. Like the homeless who fill the cavities under those covered overhangs of New York City skyscrapers, or the pretzel vendors who stand sentry at each midtown street corner, it was just another interruption to studiously ignore as one meandered through the city. New Yorkers never look at a vendor unless they are hungry, and one has to be accosted by a panhandler in order for the homeless to gain one's attention. Those unfortunates are just there, part of the landscape that city dwellers learn to tune out. Unless the couple who seemed to be moving their belongings as fast as possible began to block the sidewalk and thus inconvenience someone, it was just another moment in the day that one could quickly decide to ignore and forget.

If you *had* stood and gawked, you might have noticed the young man. He seemed to own a lot of clothes. The giant suitcase the youth was hauling had little dolly wheels and was big enough to hold a dozen suits. Another individual stood near the door, supervising the luggage removal. The long teal Lincoln Town Car that the Ford Motor Company described as "deep evergreen metallic" was to receive the big bag, but it hadn't been parked directly in front of the building. Manhattan parking spaces are always at a premium, even on a Sunday. The automobile was parked farther down the block, near Central Park. The young man had to lug the large suitcase towards the Town Car. The contents were too heavy to bounce, and threatened to stall as the stuttering casters seemed to catch every crack in the sidewalk. Though strong in appearance, the man still had a tough time getting the luggage up and into the yawning trunk. He let it land with a thump in the waiting rear cavern of the automobile, which was curiously lined with plastic. Then, using both hands, he slammed the trunk shut. The beautiful day that was just beginning for most New Yorkers was a balmy seventy-four degrees. Because of the near-perfect weather, the young man didn't sweat after his exertions.

There was just one thing. The large piece of luggage, its sides bulging, appeared to be leaking. Small, dark droplets. Dots begging to be connected. If you had stopped and studied the drips leading to the car your first thought would have been that the suitcase was leaving a trail of blood.

The two seemed to be in a hurry. With the trunk now closed, the young man almost ran to the driver's side of the Lincoln. The green car sped away quickly, turned on to Madison Avenue, and disappeared into a blur of bright yellow taxi cabs.

Chapter One

A Millionaire's Mansion

"To tell the truth, I was born above a brothel in New Orleans," the *bon vivant* of East 65th Street, Irene Silverman, once told her neighbor, screenwriter Miki Ben-Kiki. Whether or not she was born above a whorehouse is immaterial. Irene Silverman, by all accounts, managed to live a full and colorful life in spite of some very humble beginnings.

Her mother, a Greek immigrant seamstress, married an Italian fishmonger at about the time Archduke Francis Ferdinand of Austria-Hungary was being assassinated by a Serbian nationalist, his death triggering World War One. Two years later, in 1916, Irene Silverman, then Irene Zambelli, entered the world amid the sights, sounds, and smells of a lively New Orleans, a city rife with life and baptized by water on almost all of its edges.

Irene's father had one claim to fame. He was related to the great ballet dancer, Carlotta Zambelli. In the first half of this century, the name of Carlotta Zambelli was as well known in the world of ballet as Mikhail Baryshnikov and Dame Margot Fonteyn are to the second half. A critic wrote of Carlotta Zambelli in the ballet *Sylvia*, "No one who saw her will forget the radiant entrance at the head of the nymphs . . . [she] is like an exquisite piece of embroidery."

Hoping the family genes would triumph, ballet lessons were given several times each week to their only child, the girl they affectionately called Irena.

"We lived on the edge of respectability," Irene once

reminisced. When Irene was sixteen, their grip on respectability deserted them. Irene's father, discouraged by the sporadic work he was getting in 1932—the depth of the Great Depression—gave up and he abandoned the family. Her mother, still with dreams of producing a prima ballerina, brought Irene to New York to study ballet under the famous Russian ballet instructor, Michael Fokine. Irene's lessons were paid for by her mother with Fokine costumes she made for him to order.

Irene's mother at first supported the two of them by sewing garments on Seventh Avenue for fashion houses like Elizabeth Arden. Fokine's costumes were sewn together at night or on the weekends. It was a hard life for both of them, but it helped make the petite—just under five feet— eighty-eight-pound Irene employable in the world of ballet. Though Irene Zambelli had once dreamed of touring with a world class ballet company—in particular the Paris Opera Ballet, whose roots went back to the seventeenth century— she settled for the then only resident ballet company in New York City—the *corps de ballet* at the legendary Radio City Music Hall.

"I had to be gainfully employed because it was just my mother and myself," she would tell dance writer and critic John Gruen. Irene Zambelli entered the grueling professional world of dance in 1933 at thirty-six dollars a week. Irene, the shortest dancer on the Radio City stage, was always placed at the end of the line. She did four shows a day, seven days a week, *en pointe*, on a concrete stage— torturous conditions for a performer. The first call on the opening day of a new work was at six-thirty in the morning. Because of that early start time, some of the girls who lived in New York's outer reaches would be allowed to sleep overnight in the ballet's dormitory, which had been built for just that reason. In between performances would be rehearsals. There were tough times when Irene's toes bled through the satin fabric of her ballet slippers. She would also sporadically come down with shin splints, a common injury, and have to be treated in the mammoth theater's own infirmary.

"Irene lived across the street from the theater when she

was a ballerina. Sometimes her feet hurt so much she would walk home barefoot," her confidante, Ken Parsons, editor of the trade magazine *Stitches* remembered.

"We all had to join AGVA (American Guild of Variety Artists) and pay dues," her good friend and fellow Radio City ballet dancer Janice Herbert recounted. "I remember the union man—a little fat guy with a cigar—coming around every two weeks and taking a few of our dollars. But they never did much for us."

In 1933, Radio City, with its 5,901 seats, billed itself as the "Showplace of the Nation," charging an admission of seventy-five cents at weekday matinees, and $1.10 after five. Weekends were $1.10 and $1.65. Irene debuted in a performance of *Bolero*, which was part of a package that included the Rockettes and a new motion picture, Fay Wray in the world premiere of *King Kong*. The sets for the ballet productions came from Radio City's art director, a more-than-capable Vincent Minnelli (father of Liza). The theater got all the best movies that year. Irene's dancers followed with an extravaganza called the *Undersea Ballet* but, besides the Rockettes, had to compete with a twenty-five-year-old Katharine Hepburn, starring in her first big film hit, the now classic *Little Women*.

Irene's mother also worked long hours. After enduring twelve-hour-days sewing in the garment district, she would come home and create Irene's wardrobe. And she made extra dollars by taking orders for party dresses from her daughter's fellow dancers at Radio City.

Irene and her mother were two of the lucky ones. The largest employer in New York in the 1930s may well have been the International Apple Shipper's Association who, at the peak of the Depression, would hire some 6,000 desperate men and women to sell apples—one for every street corner in Manhattan. The vendors would pay $1.75 for a crate of fruit, sell them for a nickel each, and when the box was empty, would clear a profit of $1.85.The reluctant entrepreneurs were a constant reminder to the more gainfully employed that they were, in the poetic words of journalist Gene

Fowler, "like half-remembered sins sitting upon the conscience of the city."

The world of Irene Zambelli in those days was a Manhattan of Hoovervilles that had sprung up in Central Park, on Riverside Drive, on the Hudson River, and one on the bank of East River, as described by author Matthew Josephson in a New York daily newspaper:

> It was a fairly popular 'development' made up of a hundred or so dwellings, each the size of a dog house or chickencoop, often constructed with much ingenuity out of wooden boxes, metal cans, strips of cardboard or old tar paper. Here, human beings lived on the margin of civilization by foraging for garbage, junk, and waste lumber. I found some splitting or sawing wood with dull tools to make fires; others were picking through heaps of rubbish they had gathered before their doorways or cooking over open fires or battered oilstoves. Still others spent their days improving their rent-free homes making them sometimes fairly solid and weatherproof. As they went about their business, they paid no attention to curious visitors or the slum children playing underfoot. Most of them, according to the police, lived by begging or trading in junk; when all else failed, they ate at the soup kitchens or public canteens. They were of all sorts, young and old, some of them rough looking and suspicious of strangers. They lived in fear of being forcibly removed by the authorities, though the neighborhood people in many cases helped them and the police tolerated them for the time being . . .

Irene Zambelli was shaped by the Depression. She was one of those who fasted for days so she could go to the garishly painted ALL YOU WANT TO EAT FOR SIXTY CENTS restaurants near the theater, gorge herself, then not eat for several more days in order to repeat the process. The *New York Herald Tribune* described one such restaurant owner bemoaning a man who "came in Friday night, a rough looking customer. He had a tomato juice cocktail, soup, three orders of liver with onions, potatoes, two salads, four cups of coffee, a pie a la mode, a custard and some other dessert—a watermelon, I think. For bread, he had crackers, corn muffins, and whole wheat rolls. I don't think he knew what he was doing when he walked out . . .''

Despite their arduous work conditions and the times in which she lived, Irene Zambelli, whom her fellow dancers dubbed Zambi, partly because it rhymed with Bambi, always managed to stay an optimist. It was Zambi who, among the hoofers of Radio City, managed to find the time for pranks and practical jokes.

''The thirty-six dollars a week looked like a lot of money then. Still, I was very mischievous. I would step on the train of the girl who was walking in front of me, bad little things like that,'' she once remembered with a giggle.

In her later years, she would become annoyed when people she met assumed she had been a member of the high-kicking Rockettes and not a ballerina.

''She wanted to make it clear it was more than a chorus line, and that it had a patina of civilization,'' Ronald Griele of New York's Columbia University explained.

''Some of it was for the masses and was a little bit corny,'' her friend Janice Herbert would tell the *New York Times*. ''But some of it was magnificent.''

The *corps de ballet* alternated on stage with the Rockettes in the 1930s, performing classical ballet while the chorus girls of the Rockettes did many of the same famous routines for which they are still renowned today.

After ten years of the Radio City Music Hall grind, Irene Zambelli let a man, a decade older than she, enter her life. His name was Samuel Silverman and he was a real-estate executive on the rise.

''Whatever reservations I had were overcome by the realization he was going to make me rich,'' Irene recalled years later. ''It was going to be a marriage of convenience for us both.''

Sam, who had fixed his eyes upon Irene one night as she danced on Radio City's mammoth stage, had fallen in love with her at first sight. He began showing up when the curtain came down just to escort her home. Samuel Silverman, friends say, was smitten.

"He was her Stage Door Johnny," remembers a confidant of the two, Hawaiian real-estate tycoon Stuart Ho. "Irene was bright and bubbly, an Auntie Mame type, but she still could be serious. He was brilliant, with connections at the highest level."

Irene once joked that "with a Greek mother and an Italian father I'd better do something about [my name]. So I anglicized it by marrying a Jew."

Irene and Sam were married in 1941 in a synagogue around the corner from Radio City Music Hall. Zambi's new husband gave her a generous wedding gift: He agreed to let her mother live with them. He didn't have a choice, really. Irene simply said, "She's part of the deal." Sam had been married before and had two sons from that union whom Irene detested. They never had children of their own. But they soon had money, lots of it.

Sam was then with Empire Trust, one of Manhattan's larger banks. It was only a matter of time before the entrepreneurial Sam founded his own firm. Sam Silverman began to make his millions after World War Two. Versatile, he made financial killings on both the low end and the high end of real estate, becoming a slum landlord in Brooklyn and Harlem, while operating as a "hound dog," as Stuart Ho described his old friend, for Columbia University.

"Columbia trusted him to sniff out the properties. Then the school would [use its endowment funds to] finance them and Sam would get a finder's fee," Ho remembered.

Sam soon began to use his real estate know-how all around the world, primarily concentrating on Hawaii and France. He advised Los Angeles movie-theater chain mogul William Forman on property acquisitions. In Hawaii, he was the advisor to Hawaiian business magnate Chinn Ho, Stuart Ho's father. Irene was the model corporate wife, using her New Orleans self-taught Cajun French to charm Parisians, while making time to attend productions by the great opera and ballet companies of Europe. Sam and Irene enjoyed a grand life. They owned an apartment in Honolulu and another in the City of Lights that backed onto a musical cabaret theater, where they could hear the plays being sung and performed while they lay in bed at night.

In 1957, they made their ultimate personal purchase, the magnificent five-story beaux arts mansion with the great carved stone face above its front door. It had been originally built for New York City tycoon William Gussow and his family in 1881. Around the time that the nineteenth century became the twentieth, a limestone facade was added by a new owner, developer W. T. Hall. Throughout the century various residents had added extensions and alterations, fine-tuning it to their tastes.

If real estate is all about location, Sam and Irene had probably chosen the ultimate New York City address, which bespoke money and power. Actor-comedian Bill Cosby would live close by. The Giorgio Armani clothing salon, with its $2000 men's suits, made its New York home on the corner of Madison Avenue and East 65th Street, fifty steps away. Valentino's boutique was across the street from Armani, and Central Park buffered the other end of Irene and Sam's block. Their neighborhood synagogue, Temple Emanu-el, would become so fashionable that the Prime Minister of Israel, Benjamin Netanyahu, attended when visiting the city. The consulates of Pakistan, India, and the Congo— all within a block—added more stability. And many of the city's best, nontouristy restaurants were within a five-minute stroll. The gourmet shop next door epitomized what the neighborhood's residents took for granted as staples in their lives. The lettering on the discreetly worded awning said it all: *Truffles and Caviar*.

After buying the five-story mansion, Irene began fashioning the house as a grand salon of the arts. She didn't worry about the opinions of others. Better to be *nouveau riche* than *nouveau* poor, was her motto. Eclectic to the extreme, she hung a Renoir in the bathroom and a large painting of herself wearing a ballerina's tutu in the library. She placed an old pair of pink ballet slippers she had once danced in on a small round maple table and surrounded the shoes with cactus plants.

Their home had a small two-person elevator that went from the first floor to the roof terrace, where Irene eventually let a rooftop garden dominate. The garden was partly to let her favorite exotic flowers—white gardenias and orchids—feel the summer heat. One prized gardenia plant would bloom several times each year for over a decade. She used the mansion's roof to the fullest, finding room to keep three or four cats on top of it and to grow vegetables—tomatoes and herbs. Each year, she tied the tomatoes to the formidable spear-pointed wrought iron fence that kept potential thugs from having any chance of entering her home from above. On most evenings, the roof garden glowed. For added safety, Irene kept it lighted all night.

A walled-in back garden off the first floor allowed for a large tree and more blooms. Irene once told a visitor that her rococo decorating style had been inspired by a visit she had made to the palace of Versailles. The couple employed ten servants to take care of them, the house, and their two boxer dogs.

Sam and Irene had one more wonderful decade together after they bought the mansion. In 1970, he was diagnosed with non-Hodgkin's lymphoma, a type of cancer. Sam was sixty-seven when he died of the disease in 1973, leaving nearly everything to Irene, with a few pieces of real estate going to Columbia University. Neither of them had siblings and they never had children together. Irene's mother, who outlived Sam, would herself last past her ninetieth birthday, succumbing in the early 1980s, leaving Irene alone with her dogs and the roof cats.

Perhaps people thought the woman who was once called Irena, then Zambi, and finally respectfully addressed as a proper grande dame with the title of Mrs. Silverman, would fade away slowly. Maybe they expected her to rattle around her mansion like a Manhattan Norma Desmond with only an old male caretaker to dab drool from the corners of her lips. If so, they were mistaken. After Sam died, Irene Silverman, always a survivor, once more began to quicken the pace of her life.

She started by dividing the already compartmentalized mansion into a deluxe extended-stay bed and breakfast, cultivating the rich and famous who were visiting New York. Her remodeling plan created nine suites of varying sizes, many with marble fireplaces and floors. Some could truly be termed apartments, while others were simply oversized rooms. Irene kept a first-floor office for herself, and on the second floor there was a large living room, kitchen, and bedroom.

Zambi always said it wasn't just for the money. She wanted the company of interesting people. Real-estate agents steered clients to her door and the favorable word-of-mouth kept her home full. She always checked their references; Dina Andrew of the Feathered Nest realty firm did it for her. Andrew told friends Irene "prided herself on judging people's character."

"If she liked her guest, she'd have the servants bring him breakfast in bed," said Ben-Kiki. "And if she *really* liked you, she'd take *you* out to dinner."

"It [the mansion] was always a work in progress," a tenant, Henry Sinkel, recalled. "Something was always being puffed, fluffed, renovated, and changed. You never knew when you walked in if something wasn't being fine-tuned."

And, although she had millions, there was still that Depression mentality of hers, rarely turning down a dollar tendered. Ben-Kiki said that, on a few rare occasions when the home was filled, the former ballerina would give up her own second-floor apartment to a regular tenant, take a dog into the basement, and sleep on a small single bed near the wine cellar with nothing but bare lightbulbs for illumination. Yet Irene hooted when anyone suggested she was doing it for the cash.

"You think this is about money? It's not," she indignantly huffed to a friend who suggested otherwise.

Even before Sam died, Irene Silverman had decided to fill in many of the gaps in her education. She enrolled in classes at Columbia University, mostly art and drawing sessions. She was quite good at portraits, preferring to draw herself. Inevitably, a self-portrait she created would hang behind the door to her office, while smaller drawings and photos of herself crowded her desk.

The younger students—they were all younger—looked upon her as a curiosity. Irene was filthy rich and she didn't try to hide it for a minute. Most days she arrived at Columbia by limousine, often keeping the driver waiting for hours as she took her classes.

The university classes were a success. After Sam passed away, Irene replaced the art courses with history studies, where she became the most popular person in her student group. Following a lecture it would be Irene Silverman who would order in exquisite catered lunches or marry a selection of exotic aged cheeses and fruit with vintage wines from her cellar to share with the other students. She always kept a small split of her favorite French champagne, *Veuve Clicquot*, in her purse, and it didn't take much of an occasion to get her to pop the cork and turn the bottle upside down.

She was a delightful, often flamboyant, eccentric and celebrities in the know were eager to spend a week or a month at *chez Irena* as paying guests instead of at a drab hotel. Pop singer Chaka Khan, conductor Peter Duchin, and inspirational author Andrew Murray were frequent guests. Peter Jacobson, the television producer who had married his star, Fran Drescher, and then put her in a hit TV comedy series, *The Nanny*, was a regular tenant.

"She kept things cracking and we had some good times," a bemused Duchin once said about life at Irene's.

One regular who found romance on his trip to New York came home one day to find his bed removed and a larger one installed. His cupid was Irene. Each suite was perpetually being redecorated to fit Her impulsive tastes, often frequently darting off in new directions if a picture in a decorating magazine struck her fancy. For the most part, both her servants and clients found her moods charming. One night she'd serve BLTs, the next, a cheese plate, and on another, the kind of silky, French cuisine she had enjoyed in Michelin three-star restaurants.

The widow Silverman also loved to dish and behave with irreverence. She thought Bill Clinton's appointed tormentor, Ken Starr, had a weak chin. Irene thrived on being politically incorrect.

On one memorable night she swept into a party on the arms of ten muscular young men she had decked out in black tie. When asked about her escorts she had a puckish, rehearsed answer.

"I rented them. For the night," Irene Silverman winked. Her quirks were becoming legend. The servants gossiped about her insistence that the nearly 300 tropical plants that filled the mansion be watered with knobby old gin bottles, taking forever to fill.

She bred her show-champion boxers and sold their pups for $500 each. Irene still wanted to make a buck, even though she had no need to do so. But, when a little girl wanted to buy one and couldn't afford it, she asked her to just give her the change in her piggy bank. When she got the small amount of coins, she gave it to the New York Humane Society.

Not that she was ever a saint. Or anyone's fool for that matter. Nor did she suffer fools gladly. If she didn't like a guest, he or she got a short stay. Irene simply told them they had to leave after their first week or month was up. Those who bored or annoyed her were not allowed back. You had to be a charmer, besides being well-heeled, to stay at Mrs. Silverman's manse.

"She had a temper," remembered James Shenton, Ph.D., a Columbia University professor. "She once told me, 'Never forget, I grew up in New Orleans, so I know what a fishmonger's wife is.' "

Irene was 82 years old in 1998, and was sensible enough to plan for a natural demise. The mansion, she had decided, would be given to a school of the arts. It would be a center for worthy students who would stay and study there. A tax-exempt corporation, the Colby Foundation, was set up to honor her mother. Its goal would be to "promote the needle arts," and research in the history of the fashion trade. She made donations to the Kosciuszko Foundation, the American center for Polish culture, which was across the street. She created a seventy-five-minute oral history of her life and experiences in her dance career. She gave the audio tape to the library of the New York's Lincoln Center for the Performing Arts. Like the rest of her life, she planned to not only depart in style, but to leave a little something for others behind.

The widow Silverman was slowing down, but determined not to show it. No gray hair for her—a beauty salon colored it Lucille Ball orange-red. Still, her back hurt, and arthritis was taking a toll on her fingers. Her eyesight was going as well, but she would still amaze her tenants some mornings by appearing dressed only in a nightgown. Irene would greet her guests in a ballerina's pose, her hands above her head, fingers gracefully pointed inward like Odile in Swan Lake about to do her 32 *fouette* turns. Then, for a split second, she would rise *en pointe*, and giggle. She was little Zambi again, if only for a instant.

There were a few more good years left.

The blue-eyed young man with the prizefighter's broken nose and the slight limp had been hanging around Irene Silverman's neighborhood for almost a month. His rich, full head of dark hair had been streaked blond, a fashionable touch for male celebrities that summer. At the bar of the Plaza Athenee, a small, posh hotel on East 64th Street, two blocks away, the staff thought the callow peroxided youth was a *walker*, a term used by urbane New Yorkers to describe handsome, gay men who supplemented their incomes by escorting older, rich women to dinner and to parties. Not that he was effeminate. The youth seemed to be virile enough. In fact, his features and his seeming inability to smile gave him a cruel appearance.

On the Upper East Side he was often seen in the company of one such apparent matriarch who looked old enough to be his mother. The two were staying at the stylish St. Regis hotel on East 55th Street and the matron and her young man appeared to be eating their way through Manhattan's better restaurants at a quick clip. After a first night's samplings of the pleasures of their hotel's Lespinasse, the two appeared next at Barbetta, an upscale Italian eatery in the theatre district. The waiter thought his aged, sagging companion could be Elizabeth Taylor. He was not dissuaded—the lady flashed her gaudy jewelry his way and smiled conspiratorily, seemingly delighted at his unspoken recognition.

Her *macho*-appearing escort seemed to have all the trappings of wealth. He drove a green Lincoln Town Car and was willing to pay the top rate of $580 a month at the Stellmar garage on East 65th Street for in-and-out privileges.

Gary Evans, a neighborhood hairdresser, thought the two looked like they fit right into the tony East Side scene. The young man dressed, Gary would recall, "like something out of *The Great Gatsby*. You know, if you dress nice and look well, you can slip in."

The tall youth would spend his mornings trolling the East Sixties alone as if he were looking for something specific. An address? A more permanent place to stay? In May 1998, he showed up at the doorstep of a wealthy older woman who lived several blocks north of Irene Silverman and sometimes rented out spare rooms. She also had some nice real estate in the Commonwealth of the Bahamas. But the owner was out of town and the occupant in the house wouldn't take his bait—an offer of hard cash. It was time to go to Plan B. He consulted his list of names.

During the first week of June, he appeared at 3 East 65th Street, a building that just missed being directly across the street from 20 East 65th. An apartment was available at $2,000 a month.

"He was charming but also full of baloney," Bob Hammer, the real-estate agent who showed him the property, would recall.

The charmer's name was Kenny Kimes, who introduced himself to Hammer as Tony Tsoukas. He was lacking in credentials, Hammer thought. He stumbled when called upon to recall his stolen social security number, then asked to use a bathroom where he took the rental application with him. When he returned, the FICA number was completed on the form.

Hammer's real-estate agency ran a check through a credit firm, TRW. The phone number he had given as a reference in Florida didn't work. The social security number belonged to a man who was hospitalized in West Palm Beach, Florida. His wife called Hammer to let her know her displeasure.

"Hey, my husband's in the hospital. He's not renting any apartment in New York," she told Hammer.

Hammer told a friend that he knew he had a phony on his hands. The athletically built young man, his hair confidently slicked back like a late-twentieth-century gigolo, was told to take a hike.

No matter. He went back to 20 East 65th Street and asked for Irene Silverman. His female partner had already cased the address by phone, asking if an apartment were available "for my boss." This time, the young man said his name was Manny Guerin and tossed in the name of a West Palm Beach financial adviser who happened to know Irene, as well as her posh society butchers, the Piccinini brothers. The financial advisor had recommended the widow Silverman's home as a nice place to stay for a month, he said. Then, the bent-beaked youth pulled a classic con man's trick. Annette Bening's character, Myra, in the classic movie of conning, *The Grifters*, had said, "I showed her the money. And I made sure she saw it." The man who said he was Manny Guerin, but whose real name was Kenneth Kareem "Kenny" Kimes, now performed the very same move, slicker than spit, making sure *she* saw it. He casually plucked a roll of $100 bills from his jacket, offering to pay $6000—three month's rent in advance.

Irene Silverman, the mark, was dazzled by the display. Crisp cash—sixty C-notes—were being proffered tax-free. How often did that happen? Only fools would actually remember to report that kind of easy hard currency to the Internal Revenue gang, wouldn't they? You didn't have to worry about a large check bouncing out of your business checking account, either.

Dollar signs formed in the pupils of her eyes. Innate greed triumphed over common sense. Irene Silverman, a daughter of the Great Depression, didn't ask for references or a Social Security number. She didn't even bother to call her trusted ally Dina Andrew at the Feathered Nest real estate agency. Instead, Irene blithely handed over the keys to 1-B, the first suite on the ground floor of the building.

Kenny Kimes had grifted his way inside her mansion.

Chapter Two

The Dancer Departs

Her new tenant hadn't been in a week and, already, Irene Silverman was having both second and third thoughts. She told anyone within earshot about this Manny Guerin. She wrote about her misgivings in her diary. Irene now wished she had never grabbed the young man's fistful of dollars.

"I'm going to talk to my lawyer and get him out," she told a member of her staff. She poured out her frustration to her friends. "He's damaged some of my antique furniture," Irene told her pal Janice Herbert about the furniture, which she said was going to cost thousands of dollars to repair. Until now, her mansion, though largely rented out, still felt like her home—with every renter behaving like a member of the family. This new resident would hardly even open his door to the maids so that they could go in and clean. He was very secretive. Her foreboding grew. She complained on the phone to sixty-six-year-old Janice. Her younger friend listened with concern.

"This tenant is driving me crazy. Eva" (one of her servants who made the beds and cleaned) "can't get in his room, and I think he's hiding something in there. He's not nice. He's rude and I suspect that something very bad is going on in there."

Irene told Janice she also thought he was doing drugs. She had been around the block enough times to know when something wasn't kosher.

"I smell a rat," she whispered into the phone to Janice.

Her younger friend tried to calm Irene down and cheer her up.

"I'll bring over a bottle of the bubbly and we'll get zonked," Janice told her soothingly. They made a date for dinner.

The widow noted that every time the man entered her building and passed the lobby security camera he would try to avoid being photographed. When he walked by the lens, his hand had flown up to his face too many times to be a coincidence. Irene also had the impression he was, at times, following her. It gave her chills.

She, in turn, began keeping track. The drama between them became that of the caged hen watching the fox. She relied on her art background and sketched a portrait of the strange boarder. She drew arrows that pointed out his crooked nose and his slight limp.

"I don't trust him," Irene wrote in her diary. "He seems suspicious."

Her worse fears would have been realized had she known that he was also keeping a notebook that chronicled her movements. Her boarder wrote down when she awoke, when she took a nap, when she went out, whom she talked to on the phone, and, especially, when she mentioned his name. A criminal expert would say he was profiling her in his journal. They were like that warring couple in the long-running *Mad* magazine strip, *Spy vs. Spy*. Except, this time, it wasn't for laughs.

Mrs. Silverman's tenant soon had some bizarre visitors. A young male friend began stopping by and staying the night. He didn't speak much English but appeared to be eavesdropping on her conversations. Then, there was the fat, five-foot-five, flamboyantly dressed, fiftyish female who had shown up, hovering near him like a helicopter on traffic watch. The trio wanted Irene out before she could get them out. It was becoming a deadly contest.

On the last day of June, her renter and the obese older woman contacted the owner of a nearby drugstore, Don Aoki, summoning him to their rented suite at 20 East 65th Street. Aoki had a notary public license. The man who called himself Manny Guerin was using a favorite alias. The twenty-three-year-old Guerin, aka Kenny Kimes, told Aoki he would be well paid for notarizing a document. Kenny said he had gotten the accountant's name from the manager of the Plaza Athenee, and asked Aoki to meet him first in the hotel's lobby where, by now, his face had become well known. Young Kimes was taking a classic con precaution— observing his subject as he arrived to make sure he was alone and didn't have auxiliary help. Aoki thought Kenny looked "sincere and friendly."

Over drinks, Kenny reminded Aoki again that the CPA was getting paid several times his normal fee. Then he walked him over to 20 East 65th Street and into the mansion. There he introduced him to the older woman, who police later said was his ever-constant companion and mother, Sante (he pronounced it Shawn-tay) Kimes. She was a few days short of her sixty-fourth birthday. He did not introduce her to Aoki as his mom. Today, her role was to impersonate Irene Silverman, in hopes of grabbing an early birthday present. Aoki thought the woman didn't look eighty-two, the age given on the papers he was to witness.

"I think she was trying to act like an eighty-two year old woman, but I think she was padded . . . she kept on trying to lift something up to make herself look heavy. I thought she was a phony," Aoki said.

Sante already had a contract signed for the accountant to notarize. Its pages transferred the deed for the mansion to a Canadian corporation, Atlantis Group Limited, that Kenny and Sante just happened to control. The purchase price was $390,000, a bargain, since the building was easily worth $4 million or more. Aoki refused to apply his notary stamp to the papers, despite the promise of a big check for the service.

"I can't sign off on this. It's been signed already. It has to be signed in my presence. You have to sign it again."

Aoki recalled later that his subject seemed reluctant.

"She didn't want to sign it. She said, 'Well, I have to think about it.' It didn't sound right. After I told her to sign it, she got hesitant."

Sante Kimes, who had practiced all day to cobble a fair facsimile of Irene Silverman's signature, wouldn't even attempt to fake Irene's handwriting in front of Aoki on the first try. Irene Silverman had developed a highly unusual, theatrical flourish over the years, which was difficult to duplicate, particularly since her penmanship had gotten shaky with age. The two gave up on that gambit for the moment. There were always other accountants who would witness a document if the price were right. Aoki said the woman didn't have proper identification, either.

"They claimed she lost her driver's license and her passport," Aoki recalled.

Irene's interloper, the police believe, had made plans to take control of the house by Sunday. She told Kenny to write out a shopping list. In a spiral notebook, between the milk and bread on the list, was a penciled reminder to buy a stun gun, a shower curtain, and some rope. She quickly called a second notary, a woman, who turned out to be less particular.

Sante wasn't about to take a risk that could unnecessarily endanger her or her dear son. She used stalking horses. Instead, she placed a call to a Stan Patterson in Las Vegas, Nevada, on July 2, three days after her abortive session with Aoki.

Patterson, fifty-three, lived in a mobile home at a Las Vegas trailer park and had done paid favors for Kenny and Sante before. When he had advertised himself in a Las Vegas newspaper as available for odd jobs, Sante had come calling. She offered him $300 to move a few possessions from Las Vegas to a house in the San Fernando Valley she said was hers, no questions asked. Patterson made the mistake of asking about the move and got this response:

"It's none of your business. Don't ask so many questions or you'll wind up dead."

Patterson kept his mouth shut after that.

A few months later, Kenny and Sante wanted another small favor. Could you buy us a few guns? Patterson obliged. He drove over to the Discount Pawn Shop in Henderson, Nevada, and bought a Glock 9mm and a 22-caliber Beretta. The Glock was for Kenny, he learned, and the little Beretta was for Kenny's mom.

Ever wary, the Kimeses had the guns delivered to another

woman. Sante said the go-between was her daughter. The woman wasn't anything of the sort, though, in truth, she had once given birth to a illegitimate son. That was in 1983 (it seemed so long ago now). Sante had confessed to a pretrial mental-health examiner about giving birth to the infant boy and having to put him up "for adoption" in Mexico. At the time, she was desperate for sympathy.

It is illegal to buy a gun for someone who is unlicensed. Patterson had broken the law; and it wasn't long until the FBI found him. They wanted to talk to Kenny and Sante, they said, and if Patterson would just be their bird-dog and point towards them, well, they just might forget that gun rap.

"What's going on, Sante?"
Sante Kimes made her pitch:
"You know life has been tough since Papa died. But, now it's going to be good again. I want you to fly to New York this Sunday and manage an apartment house of this eccentric old lady who sometimes dances in ballerina slippers in the hallways of her building. I'll pay your way. If she asks any questions, tell her you can't talk. Tell her you're an agent of the corporation."

After that bizarre statement, Patterson figured that Sante had somehow gotten control of an apartment building in Manhattan and was putting it in her name. He was sure the deal was crooked. He notified the FBI.

Early on the Sunday morning of July 5, while New York slept on a holiday weekend, her killers quietly motioned Irene Silverman into their rented suite as she alighted from her elevator. Irene, wearing just a nightgown with an old robe over it, obliged. She would never be seen again.

Patterson wore a bulletproof vest on his flight to New York City, the morning after the fireworks of the Fourth of July. Over it was a maroon shirt, complemented by matching pants. Patterson wore cowboy boots and a black Stetson hat. His weathered face and thinning hair gave him the look of a cowboy who had been on a cattle drive far too long.

The Nevadan was greeted at the John F. Kennedy Airport by New York's finest, who quickly installed him at a Manhattan hotel, the New York Hilton, fifteen blocks from the Silverman mansion.

The cowboy was glad he was fingering Sante because, as he later told the *New York Post:* ''She could easily do a slaying. She sure would have tried to kill me at some point.''

Stan Patterson dialed Sante and Kenny on their cell phone in the Town Car. At that moment, they were tooling down the Garden State Parkway in New Jersey. Despite its name, the Garden State is not the kind of country road you might take for a relaxing Sunday drive but, rather, a congested toll pike. Sante told him that she and Kenny were on their way back to New York and she'd meet him at the hotel at six that night.

At Irene Silverman's mansion, the servants were getting concerned. She hadn't shown up for her Sunday morning manicure appointment and no one had seen her all day. Sure, she was eccentric, but this was unusual. Besides, there was that strange phone call. A male voice advising the servants ''not to speak to any tax men'' and to ''please take care of her dog'' had called. Strange indeed, thought the Silverman staffers. An employee notified the police, and fingered Manny Guerin as someone who might be responsible for her disappearance. An NYPD artist was brought in to sketch his image based on the servant's description.

Sante Kimes met Patterson at the Hilton and took him out to dinner. The FBI let her. They weren't about to make the bust until Kenny showed up. After dinner, as Patterson and Sante were walking back to the hotel at seven in the evening, Kenny strolled alongside and the trio began walking up Sixth Avenue together. It was early evening as several federal agents surrounded the three while they walked through a street fair. Kenny didn't tell them who he was, or even attempt to use the Manny Guerin moniker, instead trying to convince the Feds of yet a third alias. The agents had an illegal gun possession they could charge them with and a bum check charge, too—Sante had paid for the green Lincoln using a frozen bank account. Of course, that was just window dressing to keep them on ice for a few days. There was a body in Los Angeles and elsewhere that they thought Sante and Kenny might know about. The two were held without bond. Sante was taken to the Rose M. Singer women's detention center on Rikers Island, while Kenny was given a private cell in a section of the Manhattan detention center, nicknamed, "The Tombs."

For the moment, Sante and Kenny were not yet linked to Irene Silverman.

The next day, a sharp-eyed New York City detective watching the evening news noticed that the sketch shown on TV of Manny Guerin happened to look a lot like Kenny Kimes. A quick search established that Kenny and Sante had most of Irene Silverman's identification on them when they were arrested. In Sante's purse, they found four passports in Irene Silverman's name—one already had Sante's photo glued down in place—as well as her bank checkbooks, insurance I.D. cards, and old pay stubs. Sante also had more than $10,000 in cash in her pocket, which she said belonged to her. Kenny had a knife and brass knuckles in his pocket. He also had a parking ticket stub, which led to the teal-green Lincoln at a midtown underground garage. The car was impounded and moved to a special lot leased by the FBI. Kenny and Sante's car was a treasure trove for the investigators—virtually a do-it-yourself criminal kit. Inside, there was another $22,000 in cash, several blank Social Security cards, two pagers, a Glock pistol (fully loaded), and the .22 Beretta that Patterson had purchased for them—complete with two nearby fifteen-round magazines, a box of 9mm shells for the Glock, a box of .22 bullets for the Beretta, an empty box that once contained a stun gun, and ear plugs. There was also a microcassette recorder with several tapes; power-of-attorney forms; real-estate transfer forms; a walkie-talkie; handcuffs; extra license plates from Florida, Nevada, and Utah; ten wigs of varying colors and styles; jewelry; a jar filled with pink liquid; and even some syringes.

In the back-seat area were several pieces of paper, which

showed that someone had been practicing Irene Silverman's signature over and over again, using a rent receipt as a guide. Next to the signatures were two checks, one made out for $1500, the other for $5600. Both were made out to the New York City Department of Finance and dated July 2. Police theorized that they were for a property transfer fee and the prepayment of taxes.

There were freshly stained, stolen, motel pillows and towels, and there were photos of expensive houses and boats. An IBM Thinkpad laptop computer completed the cornucopia of clues. The computer seemed to be broken, but one New York newspaper said it had gay porn in its memory.

Of special interest was a letter to Kenny asking him if he still played polo or "have your house in Cuba." Kenny, it appeared, was courting the rich. On the other hand, there were notes on how to case mailboxes. And, at the very bottom of Kenny and Sante's purported scam chain, were documents indicating they owned a nude maid service in Las Vegas.

"There appears to be a ledger book or books in which they have seemed to have listed the people they have defrauded. And there are at least four individuals who are in the book who are either missing or dead in that book or books," an NYPD source confided.

The contents of the car, the bum-check charge, and the interest of the Los Angeles police department in their arrest were more than enough to hold Kenny and Sante without bail. The cops now said they were both being held in "protective custody" for their own safety.

A graying, harried-appearing New York Police Commissioner, Howard Safir, who had just recovered from elective bypass surgery, feared the worst. The NYPD top cop was told that the tire and jack had been removed from the trunk and put behind the driver's seat. The stressed-out Safir didn't have to view a video of *Goodfellas* to know what that meant.

"We have two individuals in custody who we believe are involved in Mrs. Silverman's disappearance. They appear to be a very violent couple. We are very concerned for the welfare of Irene Silverman," he told some assembled reporters from the New York press. He assigned fifty detectives to the case and then gave Kenny and Sante a title.

"They are the queen and prince of con artists," he said.

Her fellow alumna from her days with the *corps de ballet* at the Radio City Music Hall, Janice Herbert, learned of her vanishing when Irene missed their Tuesday dinner date. In an interview with WNBC-4's Tony Aiello, she said that Irene had confided in her about the new guests.

"She told me on the phone it had been a terrible week. She was having problems with two tenants and had to fire one of her maids. She was very upset. Considering who the people are who wound up with her things, it doesn't look good. She got a bad one. Irene said the guy became surly and nasty. He sneaked right past her."

Janice said Irene Silverman was usually careful. She said her friend never walked the streets of New York alone.

"Irene looked twenty years younger than she was," Herbert said loyally. "Her memory was so incredible—she remembered the names of all the girls she danced with . . ."

Janice knew her friend was dead. After learning of Irene's disappearance, she cried every day for a week.

Another longtime pal, Ronald Grele, said the chatelaine of 20 East 65th Street would have raised hell if someone would have tried to forcibly abduct her.

"Irene was not a person to go gently into that still night," he poetically told *People* magazine.

Her only living relative, a cousin, Despy Mallas of Los Angeles, was also already speaking of Sam Silverman's widow in the past tense.

"She had a lot of class. She liked her animals. And she was very giving and trusting. I hope she wasn't too trusting."

On East 65th Street police began unrolling long spools of bright yellow POLICE DO NOT CROSS tape around the perimeter of the Silverman mansion. Metal barricades were installed by the NYPD that blocked pedestrians from walking on the sidewalk in front of her home.

*   *   *

Cedar City, a town of 20,000 in the southwest corner of Utah, contained citizens whose daily lives were so removed from those of the residents of New York City that a comparison between the two might might well have paired the Earth with its moon as a metaphor. One of those Cedar City residents, Jim Blackner, was looking forward to finally getting his green Lincoln Town Car back. Sante had conned him out of it in late February and the devout Mormon and father of four had felt duped and taken.

Now, after getting the news, he just felt glad to be alive.

Blackner was sales manager of Parkway Motors, a Ford-Lincoln-Mercury and Jeep dealer that managed to move a hundred new cars a month—pretty good for a burg like Cedar City and Iron County, which surrounded the dealership. Parkway did the volume by advertising in Las Vegas and giving the high rollers good service. Who needs to test drive a new Lincoln? Just tell us what you need and we'll give you a good price and drive one right up to your door, was Parkway's policy. Call us from wherever you are and we'll bring one down. We're just 180 miles from Las Vegas, Blackner would tell the customers. In the last vestiges of the Wild West—where you could still put pedal to the metal—Cedar City to Vegas was almost within daily commuting distance.

Blackner had sold two cars to Sante during the past decade. Before this year it was always Kenneth, Sante's husband, who took care of the deal. Sante called him Papa. The old man's name was appropriate—he was twenty-three years older than his wife. Papa Kimes was striking in appearance, several inches taller than Blackner's solid five-foot-eleven frame. Most of the time he was hard to read, taciturn. His thin moustache and wavy hair gave him the appearance of an old 1940s screen star. The old man was likely worth millions, Blackner concluded.

The last time the Parkways Motors manager had seen Sante was in 1993. Then, the Cedar City car salesman had delivered another new silver Town Car to her Vegas house at 2121 Geronimo Way. The contemporary fourteen-room house, which was plastered with a lot of "Private Property" and "Keep Out!" signs, backed onto the Las Vegas Hilton

Country Club's golf course just off Desert Inn Road. It
wasn't the most expensive house in its neighborhood by far,
but the 4400-square-foot ersatz Frank Lloyd Wright dwelling looked like it was worth $300,000—maybe $400,000 if
it was kept up better. There was a maid to open the door
when he knocked.

She offered him a cocktail, and Blackner, not *that* devout
a Mormon, accepted. His customer had a dry martini. Papa
Kimes already had a glass of bourbon in his hand.

"Sante offered to take me with her on a holiday to Cancun or the Bahamas," Blackner recalled. "I thought she was
a real good person."

So, when Sante called again in early 1998, he had no
qualms about her credit or taking a check.

"I had a 1997 green Town Car she bought sight unseen.
It was a 'buyback,' a car Ford had taken back from a customer to fix some imperfections and then resold it to us. We
wanted about $30,000 for it and I let Sante talk me down
to $28,000. We took the silver Town Car as a trade-in, so
Sante owed us exactly $14,973.50. She wanted me to deliver
it to her in Bel Air. That's a top neighborhood in Los Angeles."

Blackner was of the old school. He thought he should
also go over the deal with Papa Kimes.

"I thought I should speak to her husband to tell him the
terms. Sante says, 'Oh, he's in the shower right now, and
can't come to the phone.' It didn't feel right, not talking to
him, so I called back a half hour later. When I asked for
him this time, she says, 'Oh, you just missed him. He's gone
to the airport. He's flying to Japan to open a new hotel.' "

Jim Blackner had no way of knowing that her husband,
Kenneth Kimes, was dead. Long gone. He had passed away
in 1994. Blackner also was unaware that Sante was living
in half of a leased house in Bel Air with her son, Kenny—
passing themselves off as Sandy and Manny Guerin—with
a strange manservant neighbors would later describe as their
"mute valet."

Sante wanted Blackner to drive the Lincoln to Bel Air,
where she said she was leasing a house, and call her when
he got in town. She would have directions to her Bel Air

estate waiting for him when he arrived. The car salesman didn't want to go that far. It would mean a couple of days of missed sales opportunities. Sante offered to buy him a good dinner, but Blackner sent someone else. A Parkway Motors employee volunteered and took his wife along for company.

When the Utah couple got to Los Angeles, the driver called Sante for directions to the house. Oh, she now said, Bel Air's roads are so poorly laid out. My house is so hard to find. Let's meet at the Beverly Wilshire Hotel in Beverly Hills instead. He did and Sante bought not just a good meal for all to the tune of nearly $500, but several pops of grade A liquor too. She handed over the Wells Fargo bank check for $14,973.50, tipped $100 in cash, and the Utah pair got behind the wheel and took her old silver Town Car back to Cedar City. Sante went the other way, driving the Lincoln up into the hills of Bel Air. Neighbors would say later they thought it a bit strange that she seemed to avoid parking the Lincoln in her own driveway, and instead kept fabricating excuses to ask for permission to park it on *their* property instead.

For Parkway Motors it was another deal closed. Except the check quickly turned out to be like Goodyear—made of rubber.

When Blackner got Sante on the phone, his customer promised to make it good. Sante implied that she and his driver, well, you know, perhaps had a little too much booze to drink.

"Oh, I was feeling so good, I just got mixed up and wrote out the wrong check," she laughed to Blackner. Then she diverted him by saying she wanted to buy another car for her son, Kenny.

"Do you have any black Cadillacs?" was her new ploy. Perhaps he could meet her with one.

Uh, oh, Blackner thought.

Jim Blackner wasn't dumb. And after several more promises on Sante which came up blank, and after listening to her claims that the green Lincoln was maybe a lemon, he plotted a sting operation in an attempt to get the Town Car back. He said he would trade her green Lincoln for another and she could give him the new check at the same time. Sante agreed and said she would meet him at the bar in the Las Vegas Hilton at ten in the morning on April 14, 1998. Blackner's plan was to bring along a Cedar City detective buddy, Lynn Davis, and grab the car back.

"So, we were sitting there waiting for the Kimes couple and they don't show. Then I get a call on my pager," Davis recalled.

It was Sante Kimes.

"Why didn't you bring my car?"

Blackner said they did.

"I've been watching you and you didn't valet park it like you were supposed to," Sante said.

Davis and Blackner were getting spooked but good.

"Sante ordered me to leave the Hilton and drive over to Landry's [the seafood chain] restaurant. I knew they were watching us," Davis recalled.

Davis and Blackner's confidence had been shaken. The sleuth knew the L.A. cops wanted to talk with her about a murder. This was supposed to have been simple. Meet an old lady and repo a car she had paid for with a bad check. Except this little old lady seemed to watching every move they made.

"They were setting us up, running countersurveillance on us," Davis said. "This was supposed to be a simple deal. I was bugged."

The two buddies hightailed it back to Cedar City. Blackner and Davis had gone through enough to know they weren't dealing with nice people. A few months later, the car salesman got the call from the New York cops and learned about Mrs. Silverman, who, along with a dead guy in Los Angeles the police also told him about, made at least two missing or killed. Blackner started to count his blessings.

"The people they deal with keep coming up dead," he said. "At one time I was comfortable enough with these people that I gave them my home address and telephone number. This is the kind of thing that makes you want to lock your door at night."

Chapter Three

Trail of Terror

New York's newspapers were like ants at a picnic and they didn't know what to eat first. The three daily tabloids—the *New York Post*, *Daily News*, and *Newsday*—were all getting phone calls from sources wanting to detail some of Sante's previous crimes. Snitches were calling from five states and the District of Columbia, all wanting to link Sante to mayhem. Even the old gray lady, the *New York Times*, had broken down and placed Sante and Kenny's mug shots in full color on its front page, along with an almost encyclopedic piece about Mrs. Kimes that ran on for several thousand words. The purplish prose began, "Wherever she went, flaunting her bad wigs and diamonds and hostile charm, something seemed to disappear . . ."

Dateline NBC and ABC's *20/20* were both racing to get a profile of Sante on their shows. It would be a dead heat, with both pieces running on the same night and at the same time. The dailies vied with one another to come up with new nicknames for Kenny and Sante Kimes. The most colorful was Laura Italiano's "Mommie and Clyde" in the *New York Post*. Several reporters referred to Sante as "Ma Kimes," an allusion to Ma Barker and her sons, who robbed banks back in the 1920s.

Most of the media settled on labeling Sante and Kenny as "The Grifters," comparing them with the 1990 movie of the same name that introduced Annette Bening to film audiences. The motion picture was indeed strikingly similar—an uncompromising story of con artists and, in particular, a mother, played by Anjelica Houston, who arrives to insinuate herself back into her son's (John Cusack) life after a long absence.

The *Star*, a supermarket tabloid, was also covering the Kimes case. Its sensational story, MONEY, MURDER, AND THE CON WOMAN WHO WAS OBSESSED WITH LIZ TAYLOR, was spread over three pages. Editor Phil Bunton was said to have offered Sante a million dollars to tell her story to his magazine. Talks broke down when Sante said she would take the *Star*'s money only if she could tell how she had been framed, and talk of her and Kenny's innocence. The *Star*'s editors countered, saying they would only write their million-dollar check to her if she told them where she buried the body. A reporter for the *Star* later disputed the million-dollar amount, saying the tab might pay a million for an O. J. Simpson confession or one from JonBenet Ramsey's parents, and certainly a million for Monica Lewinsky's personal tale of sex near the Oval Office with the President. The Kimes however, were only worth in the mid-six figures to the tabloid, tops.

Only a cynical *Village Voice*, the city's alternative weekly, would declare a pox on all houses. They described Irene as an "aged half-Greek, half-Italian gold digger." Kenny was a "nerd" and a "dork." Sante was his "gun-moll mommy." The paper had harsh words for the NYPD as well.

Jim Blackner was right to consider locking his doors. Besides a missing Irene Silverman in New York, there was indeed a businessman's body in Los Angeles that the L.A. police wanted to chat with Kenny and Sante about. His name was David Kazdin, and the LAPD claimed he had known Sante for more than twenty years. The Bahamian police also wanted to speak with Sante and Kenny about a Cayman Islands banker, Syed Bilal Ahmed, who had disappeared shortly after a meeting with Kenny and Sante. The mother and son also quickly became suspects in the disappearance of Jacqueline Levitz, the furniture heiress who vanished without a trace more than two years ago, in November 1995.

In Jackson, Mississippi, FBI agent Bobby Tillman was anxious to know if Jackie Levitz's name was in the ledger the NYPD had found in the back seat of the Lincoln.

"We're waiting for the task force to let us know if Mrs. Levitz's name appears in any of their books or documents," Tillman said by phone.

Levitz's name wasn't there, but the Manhattan law-enforcement team did find Irene Silverman's name along with Ahmed's and Kazdin's in the booklet. There were several other names as well. Most eyebrow raising of all was Gulf War hero General Colin Powell's unlisted home phone, as well as the classified phone number for Air Force One, the private airplane used by the President of the United States.

In El Cajon, California, the police department of that San Diego suburb wanted to talk to Sante and Kenny about a local insurance executive, Ronald Bram, fifty-five, who vanished while heading to an evening meeting on June 7, 1993. They had drawings of a man and a woman who had been seen driving Bram's red Cadillac De Ville after he was last seen. Steve Bram, Ronald's son, had gone on the Fox TV show *America's Most Wanted*, trying to find out who was responsible for his father's disappearance.

"I don't know if there is a connection," said police sergeant Jim Coddington. "It's hard to say. We're still in the preliminary stages. We'll do as much follow-up as we can. It's a long shot."

Sante and Kenny's potential hit list continued, with calls coming in from all over the country. Another possible victim appeared to be Elmer A. Holmgren, an attorney of the Kimeses, who had vanished in 1991. At that time he had just confessed to the agency of Alcohol, Tobacco, and Firearms responsibility for setting fire to the Kimeses' beachfront house in Hawaii in order to get his clients some fast insurance money. The federal government promised immunity from prosecution if he would inform on Sante and Kenny's dad, Kenneth "Papa" Kimes, and their illegal activities. He agreed, and then made the mistake of going on a vacation to Costa Rica with Kenneth and Sante. They returned but he didn't. Holmgren was never seen again.

Back in New York, the police admitted to having a lot on their plate.

"It's a very big puzzle. We have lots of pieces. We have to put them all together," said NYPD Commissioner Safir.

"The hope is that she's alive and that we find her, but in the eventuality that she's not and we don't find a body, then we believe that hopefully that there will be enough forensic evidence and other relative evidence that we will be able to present a case to the district attorney and he can present a case to the Grand Jury," he said.

Detective Kevin Farrell, one of the lead investigators on the case, was even more pessimistic that Irene would be found alive.

"I hope and pray that we find her alive. But optimism is not in it for me," he admitted.

He also confirmed that the elderly woman who had owned property in the Commonwealth of the Bahamas had been contacted by Kenny before Irene Silverman.

"We reached out to that person's family and confirmed that an approach had been made."

The occupant of the house had refused the overture, he said, and Kenny had moved on to Irene Silverman, he told a reporter for the New York *Daily News*.

"The Kimeses apparently targeted wealthy people whose identities and names they got from social records—you know, the society page. These people were not interested in fleecing poor people," he said.

It was a very big puzzle. Kenny and Sante Kimes weren't helping either. They had already hired, fired, and rehired attorneys. Their first lawyer was Elliot Fuld of the Bronx. He had departed after forty-eight hours. Now, the Kimeses had a new legal team, Matthew Weissman and Jose A. Muniz. The pair were doing everything they could to point the finger of suspicion away from Sante and Kenny. Weissman said that federal agents who visited Sante and Kenny had beaten her. Sante had told him it was with a New York phone book during an "intense interrogation." Muniz told the New York press that Sante had complained that they hit her with the book in places that wouldn't make marks. Another version said that the cops had gotten frustrated with

Sante's repeated refusals to answer their questions and had thrown a thick city directory in the direction of her head. The NYPD yawned and said if Sante wanted to press charges, they would investigate. She didn't.

The cops certainly kept trying to get her to talk. They got the same answer from Sante after every question.

"I cannot divulge the answer to you at this time," she would say primly after each query.

Muniz and Weissman held an audacious press conference in front of Irene Silverman's mansion on July 13, six days after the rich widow's disappearance and the Kimeses' bad check arrest. Muniz said that the guns found in the Kimeses' Lincoln belonged to Stan Patterson. And, he said that Irene Silverman wasn't such a wonderful lady after all and that a member of her staff may have done her in, not the Kimeses, who were being framed.

"She was not a nice person," Weissman said to reporters. He was flanked by Muniz.

"She's a tough lady. She treats her help very roughly. She's hard on her employees and has lots of arguments with them. She is not the lovely, eccentric lady who was devoted to the arts."

With Irene's reputation thus impugned, Muniz pointed the finger to an inside job.

"It's possible that one of her employees may have done this to her and is responsible for her disappearance."

Muniz told the press his clients were innocent.

"They are not murderers."

Not even con artists?

"That's a very strong term. It's unfortunate they're being roasted and found guilty."

"Demonized, I think is a better word," Weissman added.

"How many people have they killed?" asked Keith Morrison of NBC's *Dateline*.

"As far as I can see, none," answered Muniz.

"They didn't kill Mr. Kazdin?"

"That's correct. They categorically deny that. People have records. That doesn't make them murderers."

Weissman seemed to suggest that it may have been Stan

Patterson who did David Kazdin in on March 14. He said Patterson was very close to Kazdin.

"They gambled together in Las Vegas and whether the FBI put the heat on him and he found it appropriate to pass the buck to our clients, we'll find out down the line," he said.

The incredulous reporters kept asking questions.

"They did not kill Mrs. Silverman?"

"That's right."

"They did not kill the banker in the Bahamas?"

"That's correct."

"They set fire to their houses though?"

"They have unequivocally denied that they set fire to their houses."

Muniz also seemed to think Sante and Kenny were pretty wonderful people. He seemed anxious to go to dinner with them.

"I found them very engaging, intelligent, a sense of humor, you know. Just like any other person that you would meet at a party in that respect."

Their lawyers also said that on the day of Irene's murder they had gone out sightseeing in the Big Apple. They had liked New York so much, Muniz claimed, that they had planned to settle in Manhattan.

As the grand finale of the show, Weissman theatrically went up to the entrance of 20 East 65th Street and stood under the great carved stone face. With the television cameras for the six o'clock news rolling, he banged with his fists on Irene's door, demanding that the NYPD detectives inside let him in so that he could monitor their investigation, and find the evidence that would prove that Sante and Kenny were innocent of all charges. The cops didn't bother to answer.

The evidence against Sante and Kenny became a series of stops and starts. There was blood on the seatbelt of the green Lincoln Town Car. The blood was found not to be Irene's. Dogs could not find her scent inside the vehicle. The trail of blood drops leading towards Central Park from 20 East 65th Street was covered with paper to prevent further damage, then scraped up by NYPD technicians. It turned out to be of human origin but had been so degraded by the sun, a subsequent rainshower, and human footprints that it could not be used.

"It was an insufficient quantity to analyze," said one cop. Police lab experts were testing the stains on the pillows and sheets found in the Lincoln. They had also found some hair samples. The technicians tried to match them with the hair and saliva they had gathered from Irene's toothbrush and other toilet articles. They had no luck.

What was promising were two splatter marks that looked like blood, found in Kenny's bathroom. The cops were so excited they cut out chunks of the wall to take to a police lab. In another room in the mansion, they found wadded-up duct tape in a wastebasket, which helped to solidify their theory that Irene was either killed at home and taken away in a box or sack or just bound, gagged, and thrust into a sack still alive, to be killed later.

They certainly weren't getting anything from Sante and Kenny. Cool as menthol on ice, Sante at first wouldn't even admit that Kenny was her son or give their ages. A posse of California cops wanting to know about the late David Kazdin also got stony silence from Sante, winding up with only a brief tour of downtown Manhattan for their troubles. By mid-July, the best information the NYPD had gotten from their captives was a letter written on toilet paper they had intercepted when Sante had tried to slip it to Kenny. Beginning "My dear son," it told him to take care of the items in the Lincoln, particularly a duffel bag which she said contained the $22,000 in cash.

The New York Police had a paper trail, blood, stains, and lots more, but it still added up to zero so far as murder was concerned. They still didn't have Irene Silverman's body and seemed not to have a clue as where to find her.

Certainly New York's finest were more than going through the motions. A formation of forty Manhattan cops with bloodhounds could be seen fanning out from Irene's neighborhood as early as July 7, peering into Dumpsters in a several-block radius around her East 65th Street address. The NYPD squad looked into black plastic bags stuffed with garbage on Fifth Avenue, then walked through the bushes into nearby Central Park and opened manholes. One tip led them to Strawberry Fields, the park-within-a-park named by Yoko Ono for her deceased husband, John Lennon. They dug into some fresh earth there but came up emptyhanded. Holding their noses, they visited and pawed through the Fresh Kills landfill on the western shores of Staten Island. The odoriferous site accepted much of the trash from the dumpsters of the Upper East Side. The rest though, was already on a barge, headed for a rural county in eastern Virginia. Irene Silverman, many concluded, was most likely to be stowed away on an unbooked ocean cruise.

With the seaches unsuccessful, Howard Safir made a dramatic plea for the public's help, displaying the just fingerprint-dusted green Lincoln to the press on a blocked-off street. He had detectives plastering $11,000 reward posters on police boxes and store windows in Irene's neighborhood. Vans blaring the reward offer over loudspeakers crawled the same streets in a plaintive plea designed to persuade someone to step forth with information. Next to the dust-coated Lincoln, a hastily composed poster appeared with mug shots of Sante and Kenny, along with the third suspect—a five-foot-nine to five-foot-eleven Hispanic male in his twenties—who was said to weigh about 150 pounds. Servants told the cops he was a frequent visitor to Kenny's suite.

"He kept going in and out and he didn't live here," Irene's employee, Harry Papaiounnou, reported.

"Our first concern right now is Mrs. Silverman and our attempts to find her. We have a lot of leads and a lot of holes," Safir said. The archivist of Radio City Music Hall, Diane Jaust, wondered why psychics hadn't been consulted.

The Republican mayor of New York, Rudolph W. Giuliani, also weighed in at a separate news conference from Safir's.

"It's obviously an intense investigation. It involves four jurisdictions," the Brooklyn-born, New-York-City–educated Giuliani said. The mayor was embarrassed at the high-profile investigation, which was making national headlines. Since being elected in 1993, he had reduced overall criminal offenses by forty-four percent, and the murder rate by forty-eight percent, partly by posting policemen in visible, on-street positions. Just re-elected, and contemplating a run for the U.S. presidency, the politician knew a headline-making killing wouldn't help the city's tourist inflow, not to mention his national political chances.

Diane Jaust, perhaps psychic herself, soon got her wish. Two students of the supernatural—one from Manhattan, the other from Massachusetts—announced their own plans to search for Irene.

Paula Forester, a New York City mind reader, said she was tired of the NYPD brushing her off, and was setting off to dig up Mrs. Silverman herself. Forester said she had been working on the case ever since police announced Irene was missing. The occult expert already had formed an opinion about what happened to the vanished widow.

"The Kimeses were involved in grifting her, but they didn't kill her. They were set up for the fall by the killers," she said.

Her partner in the eerie enterprise, who had once been named the "official witch of Salem" by her governor and then-presidential candidate, Michael Dukakis, claimed to have experienced a vision that told her where Irene would be found.

"I saw a construction site behind Mrs. Silverman's townhouse and someone stalking her from a roof," she told the *Daily News*.

The real killer, the two seers agreed, was joined by a man driving a white cargo van with a New Jersey license plate. Irene's dead body was dumped at an industrial neighborhood around the city of Newark. Most neighborhoods in Newark could be considered industrial, skeptics claimed, which led the pair to refine their readings.

When the police reported they had gone to the area and found some animal bones that were later determined to be parts of roosters, cats, and dogs, the two found deep meaning in the findings. They said that the bones meant her killers had conducted animal sacrifices before they buried her. Irene's murderers, the two psychics deduced, were followers of Palo Myombe, an occult religion similar to the "black-magic" faith, Santeria. They were going back to dig in the right area, they said.

"We're hiring a cadaver dog, and a former Navy SEAL will be working for us. There will be about twenty volunteers," Forester promised.

Cabot, who listed appearances on *Oprah* and *Unsolved Mysteries* as part of her credentials, said the police hadn't been very responsive to them, even though they had almost given them the killer's name.

"We put ourselves into an alpha brain-wave state to find out where she was," the two wrote to the NYPD. "Her attacker had the keys to her apartment. He did work in the building as a gardener or handyman. There is a lawyer associated with the family involved."

Forester said the real killers were working for someone on an occult basis.

"They were doing their job for a higher-up boss, and if they could do their magic with it, that's so much better," she added mysteriously.

Both the police and Sante and Kenny's lawyers spoke to the psychics but a new Kimes lawyer, Mel Sachs, on whom she would soon rely as her lead attorney, was not about to sponsor the two telepathic sleuths.

"Silverman is only missing. Since there is no proof she is dead, we're not interested in finding a corpse," Sachs told the *Daily News*.

Since the NYPD knew that Sante and Kenny had been on the Garden State Parkway on July 5, it began searching the rest stops on that road, as well as the New Jersey Turnpike. They searched the grassy median strips of the two highways, too, even the small ditches in the center that caught the rainwater. The toll booths' video camera tapes were examined for signs of a green Lincoln. Drawing another blank, they went on to scour all three of New York's airports with dogs, and then searched six acres of residentially zoned land in Mount Olive, New Jersey, that was owned by Irene.

A few of her friends still clung to hope that she might turn up.

"You never expect something like this," said her neighbor, hairdresser Gary Evans. "I hope she's on the beach somewhere or on a trip."

The closest the cops thought Irene was to a beach were the swamps at the edge of Carlstadt, New Jersey, a small town just outside New York, in Bergen County. A local warehouse worker told the local police that he had seen a strange-appearing couple in a light green Lincoln at about ten on the night of July 1, when he stepped outside for fresh air. They were parked at the edge of some wetlands, known as Berry's Creek, near the New York Giants' football stadium and just off Moonachie Avenue on Grand Street, he said. The nightshift employee remembered observing a man wading through the reeds near the shore, then stumbling out, while a woman, who he said was in her fifties and looked like the pictures he was shown of Sante Kimes, waited in the car. The witness said he shrugged it off and left for a 4th of July weekend vacation. When he returned and saw the Silverman case leading the television news and linked to a green Lincoln, he put two and two together and called his hometown police department, who passed the information to New York.

"I saw a green Lincoln Town Car. I couldn't see the guy clearly. I only saw his back. I saw the guy coming out of the bushes. [The woman] . . . looked like a lady with money. She had black hair. It looked like fake hair," he said.

Police soon swarmed the swampy area with police dogs trained to sniff for cadavers. Scuba divers swam through the murky forty-acre site. The dogs didn't come up totally dry. A German Shepherd named Boris soon found a bag containing fifty Social Security cards, with numbers that linked them to Southern California. They had been filled out by someone practicing a signature. Many of the cards had been used in states that Sante and Kenneth had visited, according to a police source.

"Somebody was practicing forgery. We're now searching for anything and everything," Detective Michael Barbire of the Carlstadt police concluded. Irene Silverman was not the name being practiced, he added.

Commissioner Safir began to give Sante and Kenny some grudging respect.

"We're dealing with what appears to be very sophisticated criminals who spent a great deal of time planning and targeting an individual, and who apparently had a lot of experience in these kind of crimes. The hope is that Mrs. Silverman is still alive and that we find her, but in the eventuality that she's not and we don't find a body, then we believe that hopefully we will be able to present a case to the District Attorney and he can present a case to the grand jury."

The NYPD now confirmed the jar of pink liquid found in the green Lincoln was a knock-out drug called *flunitrazepam*. They hinted broadly that the drug may have been used to sedate Irene Silverman and spirit her out of the mansion.

On July 16, Sante and Kenny appeared in a New York criminal court for a bail hearing. They had still not been charged with any crimes. Kenny was represented in the courtroom for the first time by Mel Sachs, with Jose Muniz appearing for Sante, though both appeared to be acting in concert for both. Sachs was a prominent criminal attorney in the city. He had controversial, headline-making clients that ranged from the Congress of Racial Equality to the Patrolmen's Benevolent Association. Matthew Weissman, whose legal expertise was more in real estate, had also been replaced. Sachs' began painting a picture of two model citizens for Manhattan Justice Arlene Silverman, who immediately took time to note that she was "no relation" to Irene Silverman.

"These two people are being held unjustly. The prosecution is making all types of accusations which are unfounded. "What distinguishes them is they've been tried in the court of public opinion," Sachs angrily began, referring to the one-sided coverage in the New York press.

"It's no secret that they are being investigated for some very serious crimes," replied Judge Silverman. "There is no dispute that these people are fugitives and no dispute that they have used aliases.''

Sachs said Sante and Kenny used aliases because they were afraid for their safety. Unnamed people were trying to either sue them or kill them. He attempted to make it sound as if it were a normal everyday precaution anyone would take against such acts.

Their lawyer told the court that the two had been attending mass at St. Patrick's Cathedral in New York regularly until their unfortunate arrest. Kenny, himself, had once been a choirboy. He had also been a volunteer at a hospice that served the elderly, and those who were terminally ill. He was a website designer whose last creation had been ''cigarbiz.com'' which, unfortunately, was now inactive. The studious young man, he said, had also been a stellar student for several years at the University of California at Santa Barbara.

And Sante? Why, Sante was a hard worker for the Salvation Army who ''provided services for the less fortunate,'' and whose only desire in life was to write children's books.

''She's a housewife, '' Sachs said. In an attempt to curry sympathy he told how she also suffered from painful arthritis.

Sante and Kenny whispered to each other during the proceedings as if they were sweethearts. Sante occasionally looked away from the judge and gazed adoringly at her son. What sort of psychosexual dynamics were going on there? wondered the courtroom crowd. Sante wore a black-flannel pants suit with white running shoes. Her hair was pinned in a messy knot on top of her head. Without her wig and make-up, she was not a pretty sight. Kenny was decked out in black jeans topped by a cream-colored button-down Oxford shirt.

Prosecutor Carmen Morales wasn't buying the sob story. She brought up two convictions and hard time served by Sante, which included one five-year sentence for enslaving illegal Mexican immigrants. The court was told that Sante had served three of the five years in a Federal prison, and had once escaped from custody while being examined at a hospital. She said that Sante had twenty-two aliases. Then she threw Sachs' words back at him.

"The defense would like to portray them as a choirboy and a typical housewife. That is not the case."

Sachs cited the lack of evidence.

"There is no hair, no blood," Sachs said. He asked for bail of $20,000 or less.

"Any amount of bail you set will be tantamount to these people walking out and eluding justice," Morales told Judge Silverman. Morales said Sante and Kenny had no local address.

But they do, said Muniz. With what must have taken some nerve, he said they lived at 20 East 65th Street, the address of Irene Silverman.

Morales also said they were a flight risk even though the only real charge thus far was for a bad check charge. She refused to be cowed by the bombastics of Muniz and Sachs.

At the end of the hearing, Judge Silverman firmly denied bail, labeling them "fugitives." A shaken Kenny and Sante were led away. Mel Sachs shook his head as he spoke with the press.

"They couldn't understand it," Sachs said of his clients' reaction. "Kenneth Kimes said to me, 'I don't have a criminal record. I'm not even involved with the check charge in Utah.' "

Some 2500 miles away in Utah, the Iron County prosecutor, Scott Burns, had a message for New York. He said he was willing to accept Sante and Kenny's extradition to Utah or a continuation of the no bond terms.

"If they're allowed bail you'll never see them again," he warned. "They're both extreme flight risks."

Then, unable to contain himself, he offered this observation, one that many followers of the case were already thinking.

"This is like a Grisham novel. Twenty different players and five different plots. The only difference is that this one's real."

As he left the courthouse, Sachs once more protested that his clients had no idea where Mrs. Silverman could be found.

"They do not know where she is and they vehemently deny involvement in her disappearance."

Sach said he would appeal the second denial of bail to a higher court.

Chapter Four

Many Clues, No Body

The summer of 1998 in Manhattan was a wondrous moment in time. The rest of the nation suffered from weather extremes or natural catastrophes. Temperatures reached more than 100 degrees each day in parts of Texas for all of July, while most of Florida simply seemed to be on fire. The Big Apple's weather, by comparison, was magical. The summer tourists gloried in it as they lined up in Times Square for the half-price tickets to long-running musicals like *Cats* and *Miss Saigon*, where forty dollars got them into prime orchestra seats. In New York the daily temperatures were in the mid-eighties, and the evenings were a euphoria producing upper seventies. Sidewalk bistros served plates of herb-scented seafood, competing not just with the smell of success that poured from the silk- and cotton-clad winners up from Wall Street, but the seductive scent of Calvin Klein's *Obsession* worn by sleek, bare-shouldered women. The tiny tables were packed tightly with these jubilant winners of capitalism, who celebrated a seemingly endless bull market that, combined with a labor shortage, made their jobs seem even more secure. Sipping five-dollar glasses of California Chardonnay, the gossip was of Monica and Bill's affair, Bruce and Demi's divorce, and what the latest revelation was about that new hot couple in town, Sante and Kenny.

For her part, Sante Kimes, now in a special ward at the Rose M. Singer Center for female inmates on Rikers Island, appeared to stay calm amid the media storm. According to her lawyer Jose Muniz, she was "shocked" about her portrayal in the press. She didn't care so much about her own welfare, Muniz claimed. She claimed to be more worried about how her dear twenty-three-year-old boy, Kenny, was holding up.

"She's more concerned for her son's well-being, how her son is doing. She wants to make sure he's okay. She constantly worries about him," Muniz told Alice McQuillan of the *Daily News*.

The prisoner spent her days placidly strolling the exercise yard, corresponding by letter with Kenny, or visiting the law library. Kenny was writing back at least. One note she received read in part:

> *Dearest mom: Just take care of yourself. I know the truth will come out to the world. God is protecting us. We must be strong and know he's holding our hands . . .*

Sante was housed with just five other women. Each was notorious. One was Betsy Ramos, who was charged with helping her lover shoot NYPD patrolman Anthony Mosomillo only weeks before Sante was arrested. Another cellmate was Ruby Owen, arrested and accused of tossing her two-year-old grandchild off a city rooftop in March 1998.

Compared with others in the prison, Sante was living in luxury. Rikers Island was a city within a city. With 20,000 inhabitants, it was the world's most populous jail. She was lucky to be so isolated from the general population. Rikers was not a nice place to live. Statistics showed that 20 percent of its population harbored the HIV virus. Some twenty-five percent were estimated to test positive for tuberculosis. Nearly three out of four were there for drug-related crimes.

While Sante was in the VIP ward, there were also separate sections for pregnant women and gay men. The special segregation accorded Sante and others came at a high expense to the city of New York. It cost the city more per night to house her than it would have been to put her up at the Waldorf-Astoria hotel.

Rikers was a violent place as well. Among the general prison population, random beatings by guards were routine occurences. Broken bones and ruptured eardrums were part of the price paid by the incarcerated unfortunates, ninety percent of whom lacked a high school education. For these mostly illiterate masses, Rikers Island was home and, for most of them, a place they would return to again and again throughout their lives.

Sante's son, who had his own cell at the Manhattan detention center, was also isolated. He was in a section with twenty-two other men. Yet, according to the guards who watched him, he seemed not to have a care in the world.

"Kenny is very cordial. He gets along well," one said. "He talks a lot about missing his mother. He doesn't seem troubled. You wouldn't think he has any problems, from the way he acts."

But, said his attorney Mel Sachs, Kenny was also perturbed at his portrayal by the city's media.

"He feels that the public doesn't really know who he is. He wants them to know that he has always worked and he's a gentleman."

Sante and Kenny had every right to appear confident at that point. Despite the mountain of evidence found in their car, nothing seemed to be quite sticking in New York City's zeal to charge them with murder. And, Irene Silverman's body had yet to be found, making a capital charge difficult, though far from impossible.

The pink jar of liquid believed to be the knock-out drug *flunitrazepam* was said to be so moldy and old that it probably had lost its potency. The syringes in the car were still in their plastic wrappers, and no used ones had been found.

Another device that could have provided valuable clues, the mansion's security cameras, were found to be tin watchdogs, nonexistent. There was no outside camera as first reported, and replacement of the videotapes in the inside lobby had been performed spottily. It was another budget item on which Irene had apparently chosen to skimp. A report published by the *New York Times*, which said that Kenny and Irene had argued loudly just before she disappeared, was also declared to be false. The cops *had* found a dismembered gunshot victim in the Bronx, but the hair samples didn't match the hair taken from the brush that the police had taken from Irene's bathroom.

"I'm not surprised," said a increasingly smug Jose Muniz. "This case has everything except evidence. It doesn't exist."

The Muniz-Sachs team decided to become aggressive. They hired Les Levine, a high-profile private investigator who had a reputation for being publicity hungry, in an effort, they said, to find, in words eerily reminiscent of O. J. Simpson, what *really* happened to Irene Silverman.

Levine, the Brooklyn-born son of a jeweler, had graduated from the debt collection business to become a flamboyant private dick. The gumshoe drove in from his Long Island home in a white Jaguar that had "LES PI" vanity plates. Levine most recently had worked on the defense of the basketball announcer Marv Albert, who had been accused of severely biting a woman's back while in the throes of passion. The private eye had wired a cabby, who then recorded Albert's accuser, Vanessa Perhach, saying she would give the taxi driver $50,000 and a new car if he would lie for her. The disclosure looked like a winner until another woman came forward, saying Marv had made a pass at her while wearing women's white panties and a garter belt. The sportscaster pleaded guilty after that, his lawyer Roy Black fearing the second woman was just the beginning of a parade of similar witnesses.

"I've been known to sit in the courtroom and have tears streaming down when the guilty plea comes in," he told the *New York Times*' reporter, Joyce Wadler. "I was very upset when Marv Albert made his guilty plea. Very, very upset."

Levine, who normally got $175 for sixty minutes of his time, torpedoed speculation that Muniz and Sachs were working for the publicity they would get from defending Sante and Kenny, and taking their chances on payment later. With Levine's clock ticking, the press reasoned that the Kimeses must have had some serious cash stashed away. They did. Sante had already dipped into a bank account on the Caribbean island of Antigua, where she had a $110,000 balance. Mrs. Kimes had slapped $30,000 of that stash into Muniz and Sachs' outstretched palms.

The investigator was currently working for Gurmeet Singh Dhinsa, a gas-station-chain owner who was accused of paying a pair of hitmen to kill a former employee; and Justin Volpe, a city cop charged with anally sodomizing a black man, Albert Louima, with his nightstick in a police precinct bathroom while Louima was under arrest. In the past, he had done work for Oliver Jovanic, a Columbia University doctoral candidate who was later termed the cybersex rapist. Jovanic was eventually convicted of kidnapping and raping a student he had met in an Internet chat room. Levine had also worked for nightclub owner Peter Gatien, who had been acquitted of drug charges; and Alec Wildenstein, the art dealer, who had been sued for millions in a divorce suit by his wife, Jocelyne. She had become famous, partly because she had her face purposely distorted by plastic surgeons to resemble a jungle cat.

"That's interesting," a reporter whispered at the press conference introducing Levine. He noted that Alec Wildenstein's art gallery was less than a block away from Irene's mansion. Other bizarre cases looked into by Levine included boxer George Foreman's allegation that a fight he had lost in Atlantic City to journeyman Shannon Briggs was fixed. He had also investigated the background of model Marla Hanson, who had had her face disfigured by a hitman on the orders of an admirer she had rejected.

Sachs, who introduced the private detective, said that Sante and Kenny were very anxious to find out what had become of Irene Silverman. He began his speech by comparing his clients to Richard Jewell, the security guard who had been suspected of detonating a bomb in Atlanta during the 1996 Olympics. Jewell was a suspect for eighty-eight days, until the FBI ruled him out.

"The Kimeses also want to find out what did happen. The Kimeses are also in pain and they share the pain of us all."

Levine then added, "It's not uncommon for law enforcement to focus on one particular individual and ignore other facts. We might have to find out what happened to Mrs. Silverman. I think they should broaden the investigation."

Sachs concluded darkly, "Irene Silverman knew people who would benefit from her disappearance."

When a reporter asked Levine how Sante Kimes happened to have Mrs. Silverman's passport in her possession when she was arrested, the legal team's sleuth had a ready answer.

"Often people who work for me or my lady friends have my passport in their possession. That's one scenario."

He also had good things to say about Sante and Kenny.

"Mrs. Kimes is very pleasant, very personable, a very caring mother. Her son appears to be a very decent kid. There are other people that my office is looking into, who perhaps have greater motive."

Levine told the press that "you don't get to be eighty-two without making a couple of enemies." That gave one rival detective a fit of apoplexy: Beau Dietl, a former homicide detective, ridiculed Levine's argument.

"To say this lady had a lot of enemies . . . well she's eighty-two, how many enemies can she have? Her grocery boy if she didn't give him a tip?"

Brushing aside criticism, Levine booked flights to California and the Commonwealth of the Bahamas to find the "real killers."

Noting the attractiveness of the venues, Sachs also began planning what he called a "fact-finding mission" to Grand Cayman Island and the Commonwealth of the Bahamas as well. But, first, he had to do a celebrity Internet chat for ABC television. Muniz stayed home, vowing to file a civil suit against the NYPD, saying that the police had taken personal items from the Kimeses' Lincoln.

Sante's $30,000 up-front deposit she had given to her New York lawyers was disappearing faster than if she had spent an afternoon at Belmont Park betting longshots.

Possibly the most damning evidence against Sante and Kenny came from their legal team's own hands. Tipped off, another private detective hired by Muniz and Sachs, Lawrence Frost, recovered a black gym bag owned by the Kimeses from the checkroom of the Plaza Hotel in late July. Kenny had checked it with a bellhop just hours before being arrested on July 5. Frost held it for twenty-four hours, then gave it to Jose Muniz, who notified the New York District Attorney's Office in the apparent belief that handing it over would give their clients the privilege of Fifth Amendment protection if the cops used anything in the bag against them. The prosecutors immediately subpoenaed the bag. If Sante and Kenny's lawyer's thought they could keep the contents confidential, they were naive. While Manhattan Supreme Court Justice Herbert Adlerberg did impose a gag order, it was less than a day before the damning items found in the bag began leaking out in New York's newspapers.

Actually, the police could have had the bag weeks ago. They had found the claim-check stub in Sante's purse on July 5, and had come to the Plaza to collect it. The employees told them they couldn't find the bag and the cops gave up.

"We acted in a responsible manner [by] turning it over," Muniz said.

Brushing the gag order aside, the press quickly reported the inventory of the bag: a forged notarized deed to Irene Silverman's home, another .22 caliber gun, several pieces of paper with the name of David Kazdin written on them, and two notebooks that chronicled Mrs. Silverman's comings and goings.

Most chilling was the found to-do list containing this note-to-self: "Get a trunk with wheels."

There were also some plastic handcuffs, a receipt for a California rental storage room, two different Florida driver's licenses (both in Kenny's name), Sante Kimes' purported birth certificate, several more passports, and several pieces of other people's identification.

The items inside the bag—now revealed in detail—enabled law enforcement agencies to get the court's okay to run a ballistics test on the .22 caliber pistol. Sante and Kenny's lawyers howled, but a court ruled in favor of the tests, while at the same time ruling that Sante's defense team could at least try to block the bag's components from being used as evidence at trial. Mel Sachs complained that the city's cops had leaked so much information that they had already violated the secrecy of the Manhattan grand jury's proceedings. He said that had tainted the Kimeses' reputations, and influenced any new indictments the court might issue against them. Sachs appeared indignant talking to a reporter.

"The integrity of the grand jury has been compromised because information regarding the contents of the bag was disseminated in violation of the grand jury process. The grand jury should not be used as a sword in the hands of a prosecutor but should be used as a shield to protect and safeguard individuals being investigated by the grand jury. We want to protect our clients' constitutional rights," Sachs concluded.

The New York City prosecutors ignored him and leaked some more, telling reporters that they were attempting to build a murder case without the body. They confided they would be arguing that Sante and Kenny had carried out a fraud which entailed seizing Irene Silverman's home and her possessions. Such fraud, they said, would also necessitate taking the widow's life.

On July 24, Sante spent her sixty-fourth birthday by taking turns with Kenny standing in police line-ups. One of the prospective witnesses, who picked Kenny out of the motley group, was real-estate agent Bob Hammer. So did Don Aoki. Then, Sante and Kenny were brought before Judge Adlerberg in yet another attempt to be released on bail. The hearing was closed to the press, despite its protests.

In court, Sante and Kenny's defense team revealed it had added yet another lawyer, Steven Somerstein, to the Kimeses' burgeoning payroll. In their legal fencing, the attorneys demanded a list of everything that had been seized by the police and the return of all items that were not critical to the investigation.

"Such a request would sabotage or torpedo an ongoing investigation. The application in all respects is denied," Adlerberg ruled.

Still, Muniz renewed his argument and, by the end of the day, won a small victory. The clothing and jewelry belonging to Sante and Kenny were ordered returned. Bail was again denied, despite their defense team's assertion that they would be more than willing to wear electronic monitoring bracelets. The court referred the bail pleas to an appellate panel of the Manhattan Supreme Court despite Mel Sachs' protesting that the mere suspicion of murder should not be enough to keep the Kimeses in jail. He reiterated again their fondness for the Big Apple.

"They love New York. They want to live here."

He appeared willing to even break into that song on behalf of his clients.

Keeping Sante and Kenny's lawyers on the defensive, the NYPD revealed the very next day that they believed one of the two had also stolen the keys to Irene Silverman's apartment. They said the keys had been taken from a supply cabinet inside her residence in the mansion. They also asked for the public's help in finding the private mailbox drops to which two other keys that had been found on Kenny belonged. One was silver, and diamond-shaped with the letters COLE and SC1 on it; the other, oval and gold, and marked SECURITY and XL. They also made a plea to the owner of a navy Chevrolet Caprice to come forward. The NYPD said the rear doors had the words "Columbia Ambulette, Inc." or "Columbia Ambulance, Inc." on them. And, they again raised the spectre of a third suspect, the Hispanic or Mexican youth, who they now said spoke no or little English. The third man had been fingered by Irene Silverman's staff as living with Kenny until July 1, the night Kenny and Sante had been seen visiting the swamps of New Jersey.

The police took the keys to several mailboxes around the city, trying to find a match with a mail drop. They were puzzled as to why no witnesses had come forward to say they had either seen the Kimes couple or Irene Silverman in front of her mansion on July 5.

A neighborhood restaurant owner, Luigi Palazzo, who said he had driven by Irene's mansion that day, put it in perspective for a WNBC-4 news reporter.

"That particular Sunday I was closed for the big holiday. When I drove down her street there was nothing. It was completely dead. The block was completely empty that day."

Howard Safir still promised to bring charges against

Sante and Kenny before the extradition charges expired on August 6.

"My sense is that we will be charging them with other crimes and certainly before August 6, their next hearing date on the Utah charges," he said. He would be good to his word.

Manhattan District Attorney Robert M. Morgenthau was also trying to close a big net around New York's two big fishes of the moment. His probe into their actions involved working with police teams from Nevada, California, Utah, and the Commonwealth of the Bahamas. He wanted to bring charges that would be strong enough to keep them behind bars, without bail, indefinitely.

"We're looking for similar patterns of conduct," an investigator inside the D.A.'s office said. They were certain that Sante and Kenny had killed Irene Silverman, he said. The U.S. Bureau of Alcohol, Tobacco, and Firearms was still putting together federal gun charges.

"We're looking into all matters for any violations that fall under ATF's jurisdiction," Pete Gagliardi of the New York office said.

On July 30, Sante and Kenny were indicted—not for Irene Silverman's murder, which every cop in New York wanted—but on a relatively minor seventeen-count credit-card-fraud charge.

Manhattan D.A. Bob Morgenthau accused the two of romping through New York, having lavish dinners on a MasterCard made out to a Palm Beach, Florida, man by the name of Max Schoor. Schoor said he had not given Sante and Kenny permission to use his card nor did he know them. Morgenthau told reporters the two had made several purchases with the card, totaling $275, between June 16 and June 22, at the posh Pierre Hotel on Manhattan's East Side, just around the corner from Irene Silverman's mansion. There were also a $175.85 dinner at the Park Lane Hotel on Central Park, and purchases at the upper-crust Chanel boutique, where Sante had spent $113 on fragrances.

The aged Morgenthau, seventy-nine, was patrician in bearing. He came from old New York money. The two grifters had given his city a black eye, he thought. And Irene Silverman was one of his own. But, this would be a tough case for the D.A. if it came to a first degree murder charge. Morgenthau was antideath penalty, and had stirred resentment with the voters after New York State had reinstated capital punishment. He had refused to ask for the death sentence when charging both a cop killer and a triple murderer. Morgenthau wanted to say more but, on this day, held himself in check, speaking only publicly of the credit-card victim.

"He's as angry as he can be," Morgenthau said of Schoor. He accused Kenny of stealing the man's Social Security number and birthdate and applying for the plastic by mail in Florida.

Summoning up a new level of chutzpah, Jose Muniz called the charges "flimsy."

"Forgery is a serious crime. I do not consider this flimsy," Morgenthau responded. He asked for a continuance of their nonbail status.

Mel Sachs saw it differently. Sante's lawyer said the new indictment was being used "for the purpose of preventive detention. They are sterling candidates to be released on bail. They have nothing to do with the disappearance of Mrs. Silverman."

Morgenthau shot back that "there will be additional indictments. We're not five percent through the case."

Irene Silverman appeared forgotten in the give-and-take between the Kimeses' prosecutors and its defense team. It was left to Chief of Detectives William H. Allee, Jr., to bring her back into the picture.

"All of us hope that the worst didn't happen to her. Our hearts tell us one thing, our experience tells us something else."

Sante and Kenny pleaded not guilty to the credit-card charges on August 5. At the court hearing, again before Justice Herbert Adlerberg, Sante seemed more concerned about her appearance than the charges.

She wore a gray-and-white jacket, tapered black slacks, a white blouse, and lots of makeup. Her face showed the stress of every one of her sixty-four years, her figure a shapeless blob, her dyed black hair so thin you could see the scalp. She was visibly upset when Judge Adlerberg would not allow her to wear a white silk turban purchased for her by Jose Muniz, and instead had to wear her hair bobby-pinned up on top of her head. When Sante noticed a courtroom sketch artist, Jane Rosenberg, drawing her likeness, she begged for a break.

"Please don't make me look like a monster. I'm a mother, not a monster. And I'm innocent, and my son is innocent," Sante told the surprised Rosenberg. She began to preen, posing for the portraitist.

"Would it help if I turned around?" she asked.

Kenny also bantered with the sketcher. Wearing the same black jeans with a clean white tee-shirt and black slippers, he complimented Rosenberg and told her of his own former art ambitions.

"Oh, that's coming out good. Thank you for doing a beautiful job. I was going to be an artist myself."

Kenny said that, once upon a time, he had planned to study at the prestigious Rhode Island School of Design. If there were a lull in court or he became bored, young Kimes was ready. Under his arm he carried a copy of Jan Krakauer's aptly titled best seller *Into Thin Air*. His charm seemed to work on Rosenberg. Afterward she said Kenny "seemed like a nice guy, very charming, very likable."

Mel Sachs further embellished Kenny's past in another dramatic plea for bail.

"Kenneth Kimes was an honor student in high school and at the University of California. He worked for Merrill Lynch and was a hospice volunteer. And he was a website designer. The people of this great city and great nation—the world wants to know—why the Kimeses have not gotten bail?"

Adlerberg disagreed, and his words showed why the prosecution and the defense were so far apart. When Sachs tried to ask for bail before Sante and Kenny were booked, Adlerberg slammed down a criminal code book loudly because of Sachs' failure to follow the correct criminal bonding procedures.

"You're really playing to the gallery here," he

shouted. "Look it up! This case cries out, calls out for remand. These two are drifters and grifters, probably hitting
every state in the union. The female defendant has used
twenty-three different names."

The judge noted that Sante had two felony convictions,
and that Kenny had jumped bail in Florida. Assistant District
Attorney John Carter told Adlerberg that the offense was
defined as "a strong-arm robbery in 1997. They used force
or fear to obtain property." He said it was second-degree
felony, punishable by up to fifteen years in prison. Carter
also reiterated that Sante and Kenny were suspects, if not
charged, with the death of Irene Silverman. Sachs looked
hurt by the accusations.

"There are other individuals who had relationships with
Mrs. Silverman. This is what the police have to explore,"
he responded. He challenged Adlerberg's lecture, declaring,
"We're ready to go to trial right now."

Earlier, at a meeting with Sachs, Sante had tried a new
ploy. Tell the press, she told Sachs, that "what I've done is
a matter of national security. Tell them that I've been an
informant for the U.S. Central Intelligence Agency and the
federal government knows all about me but can't reveal my
background."

Her lawyer leaked the news to a columnist, keeping a
straight face. He then told the press that the forged deed and
credit-card charges were red herrings.

"Everything will come out concerning the circumstances
of that deed to show they are innocent," he promised.

Leaving the courtroom at the end of the day, Sante held
her head high, giving a broad, confident smile to the on-
lookers. A deaf person might have thought that she was the
winner of the legal skirmishes inside Judge Adlerberg's
courtroom.

By the middle of August, Independent Prosecutor Kenneth Starr was preparing to grill President Bill Clinton on a
hot seat in the White House, but 250 miles north of Washington, the Manhattan authorities were worried. Their case
against the Kimes couple was not heating up fast enough.
So far, they had not unearthed enough evidence to charge

Sante and Kenny with Irene Silverman's murder. Every day brought a little more information, but the trail was threatening to go cold. The NYPD had to get another extension on the Utah extradition, until September 4. By this time, Sante was reduced to asking Muniz to plead for Kenny separately, saying he was just twenty-three and had never been convicted of a crime.

Mel Sachs took another shot at getting his clients out on bail. In front of State Supreme Court Judge Jeffrey Atlas, Sachs argued that Herbert Adlerberg "abused his discretion by not taking into consideration other investigations that have not resulted in charges." He focused on Kenny Kimes, emphasizing his "clean record." Atlas wasn't receptive to the speech and, after Sachs tried to get feisty, simply dismissed him.

"Sir, I am done and you are done too," he announced from the bench.

Just about everyone had given up on ever finding the remains of Irene Silverman. Her lawyer, John Sare, at the firm of Milbank Tweed, said that, although he couldn't yet have the widow declared dead, he had gotten Surrogate Judge Rene Roth to declare her "absent," which allowed the Bank of New York to administer her estate. If, he said, Irene Silverman's body was not found within three years, she could legally be pronounced dead. He did say that Kenny and Sante were not named as beneficiaries in Irene's will.

Mel Sachs seized on Sare's admission as evidence of Sante and Kenny's innocence.

"The will shows that the Kimeses had absolutely no motive to cause the demise of Mrs. Silverman. It is clearly shown by the fact that the will would not in any way benefit them."

Then Sachs asked the State Supreme Court for bail once more. It was the defense team's sixth request and it was denied.

"The Kimeses are being used as a doormat for law enforcement," he fumed. "All the blame is forced on her for all these unsolved criminal acts all across the country. She doesn't feel able to receive fair treatment in the courtroom.''

Sachs was a fiery advocate for his clients, even though most New Yorkers thought he had an evil, murderous duo to defend.

PART TWO

He was so crooked, he could eat soup with a corkscrew.

Annette Bening, as Myra in *The Grifters*

Chapter Five

High Plains Hustler

A genealogy expert will tell you that the first family to arrive in America with the name Kimes was Johannes Keim. He came from Germany in the latter part of the seventeenth century and settled in the Midwest, first in what would be western Pennsylvania, and, a year later, migrating one hundred more miles into the future state of Ohio.

These early, generally illiterate settlers, who sailed from Europe, also wrote their name as Keime, Keims, Kime, or Kimes. Each version was pronounced much the same way, though spelled differently, all these pioneers were from the same corner of Europe, with their origins linked by blood for centuries.

The early Kimeses were farmers, and they became part of the heartland of a new nation, rich in black soil on the eastern shores of its prairie ocean. The flatlands were so good to them that they sent the word back to the old country of the egalitarian ways of America, with its virtually unlimited cheap, yet fertile, terrain. Thus did more dreamers with the name Kimes and its variations seek the promised good life in the New World.

By the eighteenth century, the immigrants from Europe were fanning out, looking for more virgin land. Generally, the Kimes clans migrated south down the middle of the nation, making new homes for themselves in what would be Kentucky and Missouri. They took what the plains offered and, by the early part of this century, those bearing the name were driving cattle and capping oil wells that erupted from the spindletop mounds of Oklahoma and Texas. It would be in Oklahoma that the first family of men to make the Kimes name infamous would emerge. They were Matthew and George Kimes.

Oklahoma territory was granted statehood in 1907. It was among the last of the original forty-eight states to be so named.

After becoming the forty-sixth star to be added to the flag, Oklahoma was beset with a seemingly neverending crime wave. Bank robberies, murders, and kidnappings were almost commonplace. They presented a much greater danger than the dreaded twisters that annually tore through its soon-to-be-named Tornado Alley in the panhandle, blowing in a generally northeasterly direction each spring.

Legendary Kansas and Oklahoma lawman Bill Tilghman worried over the lawlessness, saying that the new breed of twentieth-century outlaw far exceeded those of the Old West. He called upon Oklahoma to assemble a special group of state rangers.

"If it is not done," Tilghman prophetically said in 1915, "the outlaws now assembling in the state will soon rival the old-timers."

It would be decades before the lawlessness was eliminated.

Bill Tilghman was ultimately himself a victim of the violence, gunned down in 1924 by one of his own drunken deputies. By 1925, Oklahoma Governor E. M. Trapp had seen enough. He issued a special order to all lawmen in the state which ended, "Take the bandits alive, but shoot to kill if necessary."

By then, scores of oil-rich Osage Indians were being murdered on their reservations for their newfound money. The Ma Barker gang was running wild through the Ozarks and the Oklahoma plains. Elsewhere, the Al Spencer gang was on a rampage, credited with robbing a record forty-two banks in 1922-23, mostly in the Sooner state.

Brothers Matthew and George Kimes were on par with any of these desperadoes. Matt was known alternately as the "boy bandit"—he had begun robbing banks at age sixteen—or "two-gun Kimes." He discovered his calling in the 1920s, eventually gaining the FBI's number-one slot on its most-wanted list some twenty years later, in the mid-1940s, after a long, unrepentant career spent in and out of prison.

How does this relate to our story? Sources close to the Kimes family have pointed out to the author that Kenneth K. Kimes, Sante's husband and the father of Kenny Kimes, was a cousin of Matt Kimes, and that Matt Kimes was a con man and grifter with few peers, whose exploits would also catch the interest of the *New York Times* over the years.

The Kimes gang, also known as the Kimes-Terrill gang for its chief partner, Ray Terrill, hit its stride in the mid-1920s. They were small boys when the territory was designated a state and the imposition of law and order did not settle well on these dusty inhabitants, who had inclinations opposed to the governor's edict. In June 1926, Matt Kimes conned his way out of jail in Bristow, Oklahoma, where he was being held for stealing cars. The next day, Matt and George Kimes robbed a bank in Depew, Oklahoma. In August 1926, they hit another bank in Beggs, Oklahoma, for $5,000. Just two days later, after adding three friends to their gang, they robbed a pair of banks in Covington, Oklahoma, in less than an hour. Pursued, they shot and killed a Sallisaw, Oklahoma, policeman, and then kidnapped the police chief and one of his lieutenants, fleeing to Arkansas. There they were surrounded, with some members of the gang wounded. Most were captured, including the Kimes boys. George Kimes got twenty-five years and Matt, thirty-five. George began serving his time in the Oklahoma State Penitentiary.

Young Matt wasn't yet ready for the slammer. While appealing his sentence, and held at the Sallisaw jail, the so-called boy bandit, then just twenty, was busted out by elements of the Ma Barker gang and the remnants of his own organization. He claimed the breakout was a surprise.

"I didn't know I was going to be rescued until my pals came back and unlocked the cell door and shoved a shotgun in my hands," he would later tell a reporter in an interview.

After robbing the Sapulpa, Oklahoma, bank of $43,000

in January 1927, the reorganized Kimes bandits tried to burglarize a bank in Jasper, Missouri, seven days later. In the small town, near Joplin, Missouri, they entered the bank by cutting the bars on a rear window in the early evening, breaking into the vault, and then stealing the safe inside it by wheeling it out the front door of the bank to a waiting truck—an innovation of the times that had been used several times by Ray Terrill. A night baker spotted the strange sight, and a posse of local citizens tracked the Kimes gang into Kansas before losing them. Making its way back into Missouri, the Kimes gang was surrounded at a hideout in Carterville, Missouri. A gunfight ensued, with Ma Barker's son, Herman, captured, as well as Ray Terrill. Matt Kimes and the others escaped.

The wily Terrill was not meant to go to jail. A few days later he leaped from a moving car as he was being returned to an Oklahoma prison. Several other bank robberies then followed, including the killing of yet another U.S. marshal by Matt Kimes. He was eventually captured again, this time while hiding out inside the rim of the Grand Canyon in Arizona in June 1927.

"I always wanted to see the Grand Canyon," Kimes told the *New York Times* after he was captured. "Well I saw it, too much of it."

With that many murders and criminal offenses, one might have expected Matt Kimes to be executed, or at least spend the rest of his life in an ultramaximum-security enclosure. The rest of Matt and George's lives, however, seem to have been spent in a series of tours outside the walls, though, at first, Matt was worried about getting the electric chair. When asked if he would escape again, he readily admitted he would if he could.

"With all I have in front of me, the rest of my life in jail and perhaps the hot seat, of course I would," Kimes said. It seems, according to published reports, the escape was never really necessary.

In 1933, both Matt and George were released from prison to attend the funeral of a sister, under the watchful eye of two guards. On the way to the funeral, the Kimes boys talked the two guards into visiting a speakeasy where they

learned that an escaped convict by the name of George Noland was hiding nearby. Matt and George led the guards to
Noland's house and set him up so the guards could shoot
and kill him with five bullets to various parts of his body.
They never did get to the funeral but, according to news
reports, went back to the same speakeasy and had some
more liquor.

A year later, Matt Kimes got a five-day leave to visit
some "business friends." A few months after that excur-
sion, Matt was given a six-day furlough from prison to go
"quail hunting." Armed with a shotgun, Matt made the trek
with his self-described "cowboy lawyer," Sid White.

The last report on the life of Matt Kimes comes from the
pages of the *New York Times* in 1945. That year, he conned
his way out of prison by offering to be a snitch on a nonexistent narcotics ring inside an Oklahoma penitentiary. After disappearing, he robbed a bank and a movie theater,
before being hit by a truck while crossing a Little Rock,
Arkansas, street. Kimes, lying in a hospital bed, was surrounded by a swarm of FBI agents, wary of his "two-gun"
reputation. He had admitted himself, using the alias Leo A.
Woods. Returned to prison, Matt Kimes never grifted his
way to freedom again.

Kenneth Keith Kimes was born the same year as Irene
Silverman, on November 16, 1916, in Prague, Oklahoma, a
railroad town carved from the Sac and Fox Indian reservations after the historic 1891 Land Runs. The village is best
known for being the birthplace of that remarkable athlete of
the early twentieth century and Sac tribe member, Jim
Thorpe. When Ken Kimes was born, the little community
had just 1,498 people. Tucked into the southeastern corner
of Lincoln County, the hamlet is fifty-two miles due east of
Oklahoma City. Founding Czech and German families
named the settlement for the Czechoslovakian capital.

The three Ks given to Ken Kimes were not an accident.
Local sources say his father was an admirer, and possibly a
member, of the local klavern of the Oklahoma Ku Klux
Klan and it was his way of celebrating. The Oklahoma Klan
was not so much a group who suppressed racial equality

but, rather, right-wing radicals who called themselves patriots. The Okie KKK soon saw Bolsheviks under the bed of any person who disagreed with its views.

The Kimes household was a large one. His father, Charles Roger Kimes, a failed "two-timing insurance salesman and part-time cotton farmer," as Ken himself would later remember him, and Neoma Brandt Kimes were both of sturdy German stock. Together they produced four boys and two girls. The oldest was Andy, then Veniece, with Ken as the middle child, followed by Hanna, Charles Roger Jr., and Archie, the youngest.

Neoma Brandt had gone to an Indian School run by Catholic missionaries as a girl, and converted to Catholicism, even though her husband was a Baptist. A relative told the author that every time a priest would come through town (Prague's first Catholic church had been destroyed by a 1918 tornado) Neoma would take her latest child to be born to be baptized by the roving cleric, under the branches of a nearby cottonwood tree.

Of Neoma and Charles' six children it was Kenneth who was first to know exactly what he wanted from life. And what he wanted, he told his family, was simply to become rich. "A millionaire," he would always answer whenever his parents' friends asked him what he wanted to be when he grew up.

The world that greeted Ken Kimes, as he reached his teen years, was even tougher than Irene Silverman's early years among the apple sellers and Hoovervilles of New York. He was a true child of the Depression, a downtrodden Okie growing up in the poorest of states, whose soil had become deeply eroded and covered with dead land. Life on the Great Plains seemed to be a neverending fight against the "black blizzards," the dust storms brought on by a deadly 1931 drought. The swirling eruptions added misery to the lives of every inhabitant in the state. Fear, confusion, and despair knew no bounds. The gritty dirt that filled the Oklahoma air didn't last for just hours, but day after day, year after year, completely destroying everyone's confidence in the goodness and richness of what was once fertile soil.

Those "dirty thirties" were a terrible time. In April 1933,

a network of southwestern weather stations reported 179 dust storms, with an estimated 350 million tons of dirt swirling in the air. The dirt carried as far north as Chicago and Buffalo, literally darkening the cities, with a gloom settling over entire states which masked the sun. One local housewife described a storm this way:

> *All we could do about it was just to sit in our dusty chairs, gaze at each other through the fog that filled the room and watch the fog settle slowly and silently, covering everything—including ourselves—in a thick, brownish gray blanket. When we opened the door swirling whirlwinds of soil beat against us unmercifully. The door and the windows were all shut tightly, yet those tiny particles seemed to seep through the very walls. It got into cupboards and clothes closets; our faces were as dirty as if we had rolled in the dirt; our hair was gray and stiff and we ground dirt between our teeth . . .*

On the great plains of Oklahoma signs began to appear. WATCH FOR THE SECOND COMING OF CHRIST read one billboard. Another was inscribed, GOD IS WRATHFUL, and yet another warned, AND SO MUST COME THE END OF THE WORLD. Given the terrible times, the predictors of Armageddon appeared to have a special knowledge.

Fortunately there were other, more subtle notices for the Kimes family to heed. Articles and classified ads were appearing in Oklahoma newspapers that proclaimed that steady jobs and a lush life awaited those who migrated to California.

"In California, you live life. Everywhere else you merely spend it," was the headline of one ad placed by a Golden State grower looking for fieldhands in the lush, Mediterranean climate of central California. Oklahoma refugees, who arrived from dried-out and ruined farms, came streaming to the state in droves. The population of Los Angeles alone would increase twelvefold over three decades. A piece of doggerel in the decade reflected these hopes.

They said in California
That money grows on trees,
That everyone was going there
Just like a swarm of bees.

Ken Kimes was nearly seventeen when his dad and mom
said goodbye to their dried-out cotton farm. They packed
seven youngsters (Veniece had just gotten married, and her
new husband joined the exodus) on the back of a flatbed
truck in 1933 with nothing but a large square of canvas tarp
to cover them when it rained. Bumping their way along dirt
roads in a twentieth-century version of a covered wagon,
they mirrored the journey of the Joad family in John Steinbeck's masterful novel, *The Grapes of Wrath*. The 1500-
mile three-week odyssey, as they stopped to do odd jobs for
gas and food money, finally took them to the fields of
Southern California's verdant Imperial Valley, near El Cen-
tro. The Kimes family then became a family of migrant
lettuce, cantaloupe, and pea choppers and pickers—stoop
work—where they busted their backs in the heat, breathing
in the hot California air mixed with pesticides, for pennies
an hour. Depending on what work was available, they would
migrate up and down the central farmlands of California,
from the Imperial Valley in the south, and as far north as
the San Joaquin Valley. It was uncanny how Steinbeck's
near-biblical cadence paralleled the Kimes family's early
years.

One man, one family driven from the land; this rusty
car creaking along the highway to the west. I lost my
land, a single tractor took my land. I am alone and I
am bewildered. And in the night one family camps in
a ditch and another family pulls in and the tents come
out. The two men squat on their hams and the women
and children listen . . .

"I was the fastest melon picker in the goddamn San Joaquin valley," Ken Kimes would drunkenly boast after he
made his fortune. The Great Depression fostered discipline

and a do-or-die work ethic within him. He would try to save his pennies, but it was hard in the dirt-poor 1930s.

By the end of the Depression, Ken considered himself a fortunate man, and began talking of his country in patriotic terms whenever he got a chance. On April 2, 1942, a few months after Japan bombed Pearl Harbor, Ken caught a bus to San Francisco and joined the Army. With his Germanic name, you could bet money he would probably wind up in the Pacific. He did.

Ken spent the war by first helping to liberate the Aleutian Islands off the coast of Alaska, and next by feeding the troops that stayed behind on the desolate isles. As a corporal with C Company of the 53rd Infantry Regiment he became somewhat of a hero. First, Ken Kimes was part of the American forces that landed on Attu in June of 1943, the supply backup for the frontline troops who killed 2,351 Japanese over two days of savage combat. According to historian John Toland, the battle in the Aleutians and subsequent American victory was important for finally forcing Japan's leadership to never again doubt America's military prowess in combat. Ken got an Asian Pacific Theater Campaign Medal with a Bronze Service Star, as well as several other awards for his two tours in the Aleutians. After securing the islands, a battlefield-promoted Sergeant Kimes became a part of the archipelago's U.S. occupation forces.

He next discovered his entreprenurial bent on the islands, adeptly trading guns with the indigenous population for fresh fish and caribou, a talent which made him virtually revered during his mess hall's dinner hour—anything was better than canned C-rations. During the frigid nights he learned to be a skilled poker player, and soon became decidedly more dangerous with a deck of cards in his hands than a rifle. Ken went to an officer and got permission to have a legalized gambling hall for the troops' recreation (and his benefit). In a Quonset-hut-turned-casino on the foggy and barren Aleutians, Ken Kimes began to regularly increase his monthly salary by playing smartly and conservatively, laying down good hands at the right time. He was not above bluffing when his five cards contained a lowly pair.

With the Aleutians secure and the Allied Forces winning victory after victory, a newly promoted Staff Sergeant Kenneth Kimes was sent back stateside in mid-1944. He was assigned to Camp Swift, an Army base near Austin, Texas. It was in the state's capital city where he would meet the young woman who became his first and, possibly, his only wife.

Charloette Janette Taylor was born August 22, 1928. She had just turned sixteen and was sitting on a bench in front of her residence, the Austin YWCA, with two other girls, when she met Ken. The statuesque five-eight teenager's mother had died ten years earlier. In 1944, she left high school and the remains of a troubled family behind in Fort Worth to come to the Texas capital in search of a steady job. She found a good one. The position was as a sales clerk with the city's famed Scarbroughs Department Store, which was then near the YWCA on Congress Street. Scarbroughs had been in Austin since the nineteenth century, and in the 1940s, was still considered to be "for the carriage trade," and a prestigious place of employment.

When Staff Sergeant Kimes drove by in a car with two servicemen, he liked the looks of Charloette Taylor's long brown hair. Ken braked, stopped, and backed up. The banter between the soldiers and the girls began, but before Ken could speak up to ask her out, Charloette, the beauty of the three, was spoken for by one of his army buddies. After a couple of dates with him, she switched to Ken Kimes.

The two became serious soon after that, and when Ken was sent to Mississippi, he wrote Charloette and asked her to come to the Magnolia State to marry him, but, as she remembers, gals didn't do things like that in those days. And yet, the older, crisply uniformed noncommissioned officer was winning her over with his worldliness and a veneer of sophistication that many traveled, decorated soldiers were able to effect after nearly thirty years of life and one war.

Charloette tells friends now that she never quite saw him as handsome. With his distinctive Roman nose, Clark Gable moustache, and a deep wind-and-sun-created crease coursing down one side of his face, she knew he had not got the looks of a movie matinee idol. But, just as Irene Zambelli had with Sam Silverman, Charloette sensed that perhaps here was a man who, with her help, would soon make them both wealthy beyond her wildest dreams. Her feeling was bolstered by the universal optimism which enveloped America in those postwar years. The nation's subsequent generation of baby boomers contained thousands who could do immediate and genuinely passionate soliloquies about American can-do-ism. It was this pervasive and common buoyancy that launched many a postwar marriage on a justifiable tidal wave of mutual hope and dreams.

Ken and Charloette were married at the Tarrant County, Texas, courthouse on February 24, 1945, with two commandeered witnesses. Charloette then made the journey with her new husband to Fayetteville, North Carolina, where seven months later, on September 22, 1945, he was discharged from military service while stationed at the town's meal ticket, Fort Bragg. Charloette became pregnant a month later.

The newlyweds headed back to California, where opportunity seemed truly golden and without limits. The magical period of growth between World War Two and the Korean War was beginning with America supreme on the world stage, as the only nation with the atomic bomb. The housing boom had begun, spawning Levittowns and suburban tract developments everywhere. Young couples could now buy cookie-cutter housing without a down payment, due to the just-created G.I. Bill of Rights. The discharged veterans responded like lottery winners, with a chance to snap up the new homes for their expanding families. Reading the cards correctly, Charloette and Ken decided to get into construction.

To save money, the pregnant honeymooners crowded in with Ken's sister Veniece, her husband, and their two children, in a tiny house near Glendale in Los Angeles County. The cramped quarters put a strain on the first year of their marriage, but they had little choice. Ken and Charloette stayed scrunched up like that for more than a year. They might have lived there even longer if Charloette had not been about to give birth. After their daughter was born, they found a place of their own.

"We were poor. We had nothing," Charloette Kimes would recall. "I remember our first job was installing a piece of curbing. We made thirty-five dollars."

Charloette said that she and her husband often worked sixteen-hour days, side-by-side, in the early years of their marriage, doing construction work on contract, whenever she wasn't pregnant.

Their first big project was a housing development in the late 1940s, near the town of Tujunga, a community just inside the Los Angeles County limits. After it was finished, they built a small apartment complex in Salinas, near the Central California coast and, in 1949, a mobile home park in Pomona, next to the Orange County line. Their first motel, the Californian, was built in Monterey in 1952. There was demand for their work and Charlotte and Ken sped up and down the Pacific coast of a burgeoning California, taking turns behind the wheel of an aging Cadillac, making their fortune by specializing in building the new symbol of American mobility, the motel. The country was booming, and California was leading the way. Lodging construction was their path to riches. They appeared to be the postwar American dream, personified.

And for many years, they were. There were two Kimes children—one of each. A daughter, Linda Jane, was born July 9, 1946, in Glendale while the couple was staying with Veniece and, on June 6, 1949, while they were living in Pomona, Charloette gave Kenneth a son, Andrew Keith, whom they called Andy.

The money they got from building the new style of motor inns seemed endless, tempered only by how hard they could work. The low-slung one- and two-story motels were popping up everywhere; the name was a combination of the words *mo*tor and ho*tel*. The noun would become an emblem of America's prosperity and unending wanderlust. Families with big new Buicks could now roam the new smoothly paved four-lane freeways, then pull right up to a bedroom door for an overnight stay. Couples in search of an hour's lust could do the same. The burgeoning nationwide highway system that made all this possible was a postwar gift—the most important program of the presidency of Dwight D.

Eisenhower. The edge-of-the-town motels were replacing the core city hotels, the outdated ma and pa boardinghouses, and the rustic campgrounds of the 1940s. The Kimes family were leaders in spearheading this new postwar building boom.

As his wealth grew, Ken Kimes was more than generous with less-fortunate family members. He built a house for his widowed mother and her sister, Alice Wardshaw, in Salinas. And, despite missing his own higher education, he was more than willing to help his brothers and sisters. Family members say he financed his youngest brother Archie's final two years of dental school.

Though these were lavish expenditures, Ken got his childhood wish. He and Charloette became millionaires several times over. By the early 1960s, they began building their dream house at 2215 Victoria Drive in Santa Ana, the county seat of Orange County. It was a two-story home that spelled success. The dwelling contained four bedrooms, six bathrooms, a large office/den, and a pool on landscaped grounds. The two were now rich enough to hire a Mexican gardener to tend their property.

"We built at least thirty motels together, selling them to operators at tremendous profits," Charloette Kimes once told a friend.

"Why motels?"

"Because it was what was needed."

It wasn't long before Ken Kimes figured out that simply erecting the new modern inns under contract was not the optimal way to make a dollar. With motel ownership providing others with near-certain profits, Ken and Charloette began to build the overnight hostelries for themselves, retaining the title deeds and forming corporations. Charloette took responsibility for hiring the managers and training the employees that ran the lodgings. Kimes, Incorporated became a small empire. They would construct and own two motels called Tropics—one in Palm Springs and the other in Indio, California's date-growing capital. They had the Town and Country, in Santa Barbara County, just outside the village of Santa Maria. They operated the Times Square hotel in Las Vegas. They also purchased large patches of raw land throughout California. Ken would build motels, and Charloette would handle the employees, bargain with the furniture vendors, get the wiring approved, and assume responsibility for decorating the rooms and lobbies.

Their biggest pride, and flagship property, was the 100-room Mecca Motel. It was built in Anaheim, directly across the highway from Disneyland at 1544 South Harbor Boulevard. Walt Disney had opened the revolutionary—for the time, anyway—amusement park in 1955 and had lived to see it become Southern California's biggest tourist attraction. Ken and Charloette were part of the first wave of entrepreneurs to see the magic and money that lay just outside Walt's kingdom as well as inside it.

A 1968 Orange County tourist brochure described it as: "Two pools! Transportation to and from Disneyland; our conference rooms accommodate between fifteen and 100 people; liquor service; on-premise entertainment; travel reservations; television; air conditioning; putting green. Pets allowed." (Today, the Mecca has been remodeled and is called the Best Western Park Place Inn.)

Despite his great success as an entrepreneur, Ken Kimes, according to family sources, also had a dark side. After becoming rich, he asked Charloette to stay home. Ken started trying to control his wife and became cold towards her. Family sources say he would no longer allow Charloette to hold hands with him, or even touch his arm in public. All of the business bank accounts and properties began to be put in his name and Charloette was not permitted to renew her driver's license. There was only a small joint account from which she was allowed to draw funds. Though she had a house budget of $500 a month, each trip to the grocery store was supervised by either Ken's mother or his aunt. Charloette once told a friend that she spent most of one day fretting, waiting for a relative to pick her up so her "feminine needs" could be purchased.

"I had worked like a dog for him and I thought that every time he socked away another $100,000, he'd relax," Charloette once said. "But he never did. Money was his god."

Family sources recall that Ken Kimes was rarely around. It was Charloette who had to teach their son Andy to ride a bicycle. Her husband, she said, wouldn't even let her have women friends, yet he himself had begun to live by a different standard, playing golf, drinking constantly with his Orange County business cronies, and spending weeks traveling from construction site to construction site. According to Charloette, he was like a sailor with a girl in every port, except with her husband, there was a woman waiting for him in every town in which he was building a new motel.

Charloette, who had been rebaptized in the Catholic faith to please him, said she never thought of divorce. To this day, she claims she believed in the permanence of marriage even though Ken Kimes fooled around on her, beginning his amorous adventures just a few years after they were wed.

"He was a womanizer," Charloette Kimes remembered. "Slick as a button about it and he got away with it for a long time. Eventually I got blindsided."

On June 19, 1963, Charloette Kimes, after years of what she termed "abuse," filed for divorce in Orange County from Kenneth Kimes, alleging mental cruelty. She would tell a family court that her husband was threatening her and, after several more hearings, a judge said that she should go home, grab her clothes, personal effects, and some family pictures, and run. She did so, not knowing that her husband had become a powerful man in the county, and that by moving out she was effectively weakening her rights to the house. Ken Kimes, friends say, then had two detectives watch her every move.

Her husband also immediately cross-complained on the divorce charge, accusing her in legal papers of "treating cross-complainant Kenneth K. Kimes with extreme cruelty and has wrongfully inflicted upon him grievous mental suffering and (b) on the grounds that during the marriage of the parties hereto the cross-defendant, Charloette J. Kimes, committed adultery as alleged and upon the dates specified in the amended and supplemental cross-complaint and in the amendment."

Charloette Kimes now believes that Ken was using "the best defense is a good offense" argument. She says when she went to see Ken's lawyers, one of whom happened to be the former Attorney General for the State of California, he suggested she be represented by a friend of his down the hall. Charloette claimed she was a lamb being led to slaughter.

The former Mrs. Kenneth K. Kimes maintains she was not guilty of adultery—rather it was the other way around. Certainly not any of the mental cruelty complaints were warranted, she says.

What Charloette Kimes also could not yet know is that her spouse of nearly two decades, and soon to be her ex-husband, was about to meet a woman who had been fashioned for him by the devil. Her name was Sante Singhrs.

Ken, the high-plains hustler, and Sante, a woman who proudly referred to herself as ''the dragon lady,'' would be soul mates from the beginning. The new woman in his life would be more than a match for the self-made mogul. Shortly after their first meeting, Sante would begin attempting to control *him* and every move he would make for the rest of his life.

Chapter Six

Sante, Sandra, and Sandy

If you sit down with Sante Singhrs Singer Chambers Powers Walker Kimes for half an hour or so, she is likely to spin some wild stories. Some may even be true. Sante might choose to tell you of the time Charloette's daughter, Linda, tried to kill her by putting some rattlesnakes in her Cadillac convertible. That's not true. Sante might also spin a tale about how she once had a husband who was a bisexual construction worker, a claim that is also likely false. Then, she might tell you of the time she had a second child by a wealthy Kenneth Kimes and had to give her son up for adoption in Mexico because her husband was too old and sick at the time and, because of that, didn't want more kids. That one is partly true. And then there is the time her prostitute mother gave *her* up for adoption at the age of ten. That's absolutely true. She might tell you she was born in 1934 or 1936 or 1937 and, depending on her mood, as late as 1946. The first date is correct. She'll say she was born in Europe, then Oklahoma City, then San Diego. It's the middle one that's accurate. And if she really wants sympathy, she might tell how her adoptive father raped her after taking her in and sexually abused her for six years, which is also false, or how her in-laws tried to kidnap her son Kenny. That's not true either. She might lie about a friendship with Bill Cosby, even producing a faded photo. But you might believe it all, because Sante can weave such a spellbinding story and look you so straight in the eye that you may never doubt a word she says.

*   *   *

Sante Louise Singhrs— in India the variation of the name Singh is as common as Smith in America—was born July 24, 1934, on the edge of Oklahoma City, in the next to the last house on Northwest 2nd Street. She was the second of three children, and was delivered by a midwife. Her father, Rattan, was East Indian; her mother, Mary, was fair and Irish. The family—cotton and alfalfa sharecroppers—whose farm failed shortly after Sante's birth and, like the Kimes family, soon made the long trek from the heart of the Depression west to Southern California. When Sante was three, her father deserted the family in San Diego, taking her older brother, Kareem, with him. Like many Asian men with an old-world attitude, he prized the male child and could think of no uses for his daughters except having to cough up a dowry when each girl turned thirteen and was of an age eligible to be married. Sante and her younger sister, Reba, were left with her mother, who had little education and few skills. Mary Singhrs only knew how to support her children by doing menial labor.

Sante's mom bettered herself by taking her daughters to downtown Los Angeles. There she soon found a more lucrative occupation as a street prostitute, working with a cabdriver who served as her pimp—the very bottom of the pay-for-sex pecking order. With their mother often occupied elsewhere and able to offer scant supervision, Sante and Reba ran wild in the city of angels with predictable results. Sante was sexually abused at eight, and arrested at nine for stealing food from a store.

When Sante was ten, she began hanging out at a soda shop on one of Los Angeles' main thoroughfares, Melrose Avenue. The owners of the restaurant, Kelly and Dorothy Seligman, who were also the proprietors of the motion-picture theater next door, noticed the exotic-looking waif, and took a shine to little Sante Singhrs. From time to time Dottie would give her ice cream and free admission to a movie matinee.

Dottie Seligman had a sister, Mary Chambers, who worked for a producer on the Paramount Pictures lot. The studio was just down the street from her little luncheonette.

Mary had worked at Hollywood's dream factories off and on for two decades and liked to tell of the time she had worked on a series of Rita Hayworth vehicles. The experience with the movie star was one of her fondest memories.

Mary had met her husband, Edwin Paul Chambers, at Paramount in the late 1920s, marrying him after a brief courtship. Ed had been in the Navy during the first World War, and afterwards wound up in Hollywood, doing small parts in silent movies, and trying to become the next Douglas Fairbanks. Ed didn't reach stardom on the silver screen, but he wasn't bitter about it. During the depths of the Great Depression in 1934, he joined the military for the second time, resigned to making the Army his career. Ed had advanced steadily up the ranks as an ordnance officer and, after World War Two, had risen to "full-bird" status. He was now Colonel Edwin Chambers.

The Chambers couple were unable to conceive children and thus adopted a six-year-old boy. That son, Howard, whose parents were killed in an auto accident, had been raised by them and left home in his late teens, entering the military. The couple's lives were full otherwise. In fact, the handsome, six-foot tall, pipe-smoking Ed, who had just turned forty-eight, was soon to be given an important position with the Nevada National Guard, and the two were willing to share their home with another needy youngster.

The goodhearted Ed Chambers and Sante Singhrs had a lot in common. Ed had been born in 1899 in Shawnee, Oklahoma, the county seat of Pottawatomie County (and, in an amazing coincidence, just twenty-five miles from Ken Kimes' hometown of Prague). He told the bright-eyed little girl a wild story of his own. He had run away from home at the age of seventeen to join the Navy. The little street urchin could identify with a tale like that. Of course, Mary Singhrs told Ed, she was more than willing to see her daughter leave the mean streets of downtown L.A. and, so, a year later, off young Sante went, journeying with the Chambers couple to Nevada's capital, Carson City.

"She came here in the seventh grade," her close friend, Ruth Tanis, remembered. "She first used the name of Sante Singhrs, but the kids made fun of that, and so then she went by the name of Sandy Singer. And then, when the Chambers couple officially adopted Sante on her thirteenth birthday in 1947, she became Sandra Chambers, except at first she spelled it Sondra. We always just called her Sandy."

The newly minted Sandy Chambers settled into the Chambers' modern ranch-style home that sat back from the road at the corner of Long and Division streets in Carson City. The house was less than a mile from Carson High School. For the first time in her life she had her own bedroom, regular meals, and a small-town life in which *Mayberry* seemed to have merged with *Happy Days*. Carson City had a population of fewer than fifty thousand in the late 1940s. The sparkling eastern shores of Lake Tahoe were just fifteen miles away, and the twin cities of Reno-Sparks— where the *El Rancho*, her high school's closest drive-in movie theater was located—were a fast thirty miles by car.

Although the drive-in may have been a teenage petting zoo on Friday nights, the 1950s were generally an era of innocence compared to the America of today. There were few drug problems, crime was rare, and sex was, at least, still repressed. The casinos of Carson City were small by Las Vegas standards, and the legalized brothels, just outside the city, rarely intruded into the lives of its citizens. By most accounts, the next five years would be the happiest and most secure time that Sandy/Sante would ever experience.

"In the summers Sandy and I would ride our bikes out to Bowers' Mansion to swim," Ruth Tanis remembered. "It was our local swimming hole. Or we'd ride horses—Sandy rode well. In the winter we'd ski at Tahoe. We had some pretty good times."

It was a good time for Ed Chambers, as well. The colonel reached the pinnacle of his military career in Carson City, becoming the third-highest-ranking official in the Nevada National Guard. He managed a company of men responsible for the maintenance of all of the Guard's buildings and equipment in the northern portion of the casino state. He soon bought an even nicer home on Division Street, a few blocks away. The seemingly model family attended a nearby Presbyterian church.

At Carson High School, Sandy Chambers was popular—

much more so with the boys than the girls, according to her classmates. Flashing a coquettish smile and flirting without seeming to even try, the attractive coed had dozens of male admirers. But it wasn't all roses. Some of her Carson City born-and-raised-there classmates would always treat her as the perpetual newcomer. Despite trying, she was never allowed entry into the most prized inner circles of Carson High.

"I remember she ran for a freshman class office and the next year for a sophomore class post. She lost both times. She never tried after that. We were a little guilty, I suppose, of treating her like an outsider," the 1952 senior class president, Duane Glanzman, told the author.

Yet, according to class records and her friend, Ruth Tanis, Sandy Chambers was as socially successful as one could be within the caste system of Carson High. She was the reporter and historian for the school's Spanish club, *Los Companeros*. And Sandy/Sante was on the school's most visible entity, the basketball cheerleading squad, in a blue-and-white sweater and a pleated skirt, leading the crowd in the school's version of:

> *Two bits, four bits,*
> *Six bits, a dollar,*
> *All for the* [Carson High] *Senators,*
> *Stand up, and holler!*

"I guess her personality naturally rubbed some of the girls the wrong way, though," recalls Glanzman. "She really *was* a flirt."

Ruth Tanis added: "She never lacked for dates."

Sandy told Ruth she preferred her men tall, dark, and handsome, just like the movie cliché.

Despite her attraction to the opposite sex, Sandra Chambers, according to school records, also became an angelic voice in the school's Glee Club. She was a delegate to Girl's State, an organization that groomed its members for civic participation or even elected office. And, at the County 4-H Achievement Day on August 18, 1950, the program shows it was Sandy who got the Advanced Cooking award.

"She was popular, no doubt about it. There were times she would come up with remarks that were off the wall and you didn't know what she would say next," recalled Glanzman.

Sandra Chambers was also a reporter for the Carson High newspaper, *The Chatter*, and, in her senior year, became its co-editor. Sandy told her classmates she was going to be a journalist after college.

Ed and Mary Chambers, her adoptive parents, seemed to dote on her. Ruth Tanis remembers Ed Chambers painting a reconditioned 1932 Ford—complete with rumble seat—royal blue for her. It was her father's sixteenth-birthday gift to Sandy, just after she had gotten her driver's license. Sandy's birthday was always a big deal. She would usually share it with Mary. The two had been born five days apart.

Duane Glanzman said that Sandy Chambers had the starring role in the senior play, which he recalls as being titled *Minick*. Sandy's part called upon her to wear a disguise, impersonating an old woman, much to the great amusement of her friends and her parents, who showed up to watch their daughter's moment in the limelight. It was not her stage debut. Sandy Chambers had already played "a gypsy girl," according to Tanis, as one of the daughters of "Romany Rose" in her eighth-grade class play, *White Gypsy*.

Yet despite what most would view as an idyllic small town life, Sandy Chambers couldn't seem to wait to leave high school. When her senior class picture was taken in September 1951, she scribbled on the back of a girlfriend's photo: "Just one more year! Actually 7 months, 2 days, and some minutes, Love Sandy."

Her classmates say the Chambers' adopted daughter, except for being a little boy crazy, had few vices. She didn't smoke. She never even drank, unlike her school chums who sometimes chugged mugs of beer at parties. Ed Chambers, an accomplished marksman, kept several guns in the house, but Sandy wouldn't go near them. She told Ruth Tanis she was afraid of firearms. Her only weakness appeared to be food. Sandy had a voracious appetite and her weight would go up and down, depending on how much of her staple pleasure, creamed potatoes, she was eating. In the summertime, she could put down, according to friends, "an entire watermelon."

Sandy's birth mother and her little sister Reba came to visit Sandra Chambers in Carson City during her high-school years and, according to Tanis, tried to reclaim their kin, attempting to convince her to go back to Los Angeles, with no success. Sandy's other mom, Mary, was short—about five-foot-three—and "dowdy," Tanis remembered. There would be long, impassioned speeches by her mother with Sandy listening passively, but, after the harangue was over, she refused to return to the L.A. streets.

Ruth Tanis remembers meeting Reba during one of those visits. Tanis thought little Reba was "short and round like her mother, and didn't look much like her (Sandy)." Reba also appeared to be a bit sullen, without her sister's flair or energy. After her mother left town, Sandy told Tanis why she wouldn't go back to Los Angeles. My mother is a prostitute, Sandy revealed to her friend for the first time. Tanis thought it was a shocking secret, perhaps the deepest one the two of them would ever share.

When Sandy's mother was on her way back to Los Angeles, Mary Chambers confided in her daughter's friend. She said she was worried about Sandy but wouldn't specify what was going on in their household.

"I'm afraid Sandy is reverting back to the ways of the street," the adoptive mother told Ruth a little mysteriously. She didn't specify to Ruth what was troubling her, but Sandy had filched one of Ed's credit cards and used it. She had also gotten caught shoplifting lipsticks at the local five-and-dime, an event that was reported to the Chambers by the police but not prosecuted.

Sandy's grades were good in high school—not quite honor roll, but close. She stood out, though, even in a class picture. Not only was she very photogenic, but she wore a smile that exuded confidence, brimming with natural assurance. It was a small student body, only about 200 in all, and when Sandy graduated in June 1952, she was one of forty-two seniors to don a cap and gown and walk down the aisle to Edward Elgar's *Pomp and Circumstance*. But, before receiving her diploma, she joined a quartet of women in commemorating in song an old classmate who had suddenly died during his senior year. There were two old standards, *Thank God for a Garden* and *In the Time of Roses*. Sandy's young, innocent teen voice joined the chorus of the old religious anthem.

> *Tho' thy grief o'er come thee, thro' the*
> *winter's gloom*
> *Thou shalt thrust it from thee, when the roses*
> *bloom,*
> *Let not death appal thee, for beyond the tomb,*
> *God himself shall call thee, when the roses*
> *bloom.*

Associate Justice of the Nevada Supreme Court Charles M. Merrill then delivered the commencement address. He titled his speech "Open Door to Opportunity."

A week after graduation, Sandra Chambers did something that seemed completely out of character, considering her boasts of going off to college and becoming a journalist. She wed a high-school classmate. His name was Lee Powers and, in the looks department, he fit Sandy's requirements that her men be "tall, dark, and handsome." Ruth Tanis was shocked because the couple hadn't even dated that long. Powers had just enlisted in the Army and would eventually wind up in Korea. Sandy went with him—for three months anyhow—before she left the marriage when Lee was in helicopter school at Fort Benning, Georgia. Returning to Carson City, she got a quiet, no-contest, Nevada-style divorce. Years later few of her high school friends ever remembered that she had married him. Sandy herself would giggle about the youthful error, saying: "It was the uniform."

Back home, Sandy Chambers took a six-week secretarial course at the nearby Reno Business School, then again hooked up with her best friend, Ruth Tanis. The two struck out for the nearest big city, Sacramento, California. With nearly a half-million more people than Carson City and just 120 miles to the west, California's capital was the destination for many young northern Nevadans in search of a better job and bright lights.

"We were like Laverne and Shirley let loose in the big city!" Tanis exclaimed to the author, reliving the salad days. "We had a first-floor apartment on Capitol Avenue, but no car. We always took the bus unless we were out on a date with a fellow that had an automobile."

In 1954, the two women were hired to work for the California State Government in clerical positions—on the bottom rung of the new Attorney General Edmund G. "Pat" Brown's organization chart. Pat Brown would run for governor and win three years later as would his son, Jerry, in the mid-1970s. Tanis recalled that Sandy, then the devoted daughter, would go home to Carson City about once a month to visit her adoptive parents. But she also began to express a desire to be reunited with her natural father.

"Sometimes Sandy would awaken in the morning and tell me about her dreams. She would often dream of her father. He was always an East Indian prince or a Hindu holy man or a king or some kind of nobleman in the dreams, coming to rescue her and take her away to live in luxury. Her dreams about her brother Kareem were similar except he was always tall and handsome. I remember seeing a picture of him once and he was the opposite of that," Tanis said.

When she was twenty, Sandy made a bus trip to visit with Kareem in Salt Lake City. Her brother was working there in a dead-end job, just getting by. According to Tanis, Sandy Chambers came back disappointed.

The two spent a year in Sacramento, then Sandy Chambers began to make noises again about becoming a journalist. She and Ruth traveled further west, to the Bay area, where the two both enrolled at a small Catholic girl's school run by the Religious of the Sacred Heart nuns. The nuns ran the San Francisco College for Women on top of Lone Mountain Hill in the Western Addition section of the city.

The school, chartered in 1921 and with just 600 female students, was on its last legs, and soon would be merged into the University of San Francisco. Sandy took writing and journalism courses from the sisters in an attempt to get enough credits to transfer to a major university. Ruth studied Spanish and English literature. They both had to take part-time jobs to pay for the college tuition, which forced the two young women to downscale their bare-bones lifestyle even more.

"We shared a room at the Salvation Army Hotel for Women on McAllister Street, just off Market," Tanis recalled. "They had a curfew for us. You had to be in at eleven o'clock and, of course, men couldn't visit us in our rooms. We had to visit with them in the lobby. I remember it was next to the Follies Bergere, a burlesque house."

Tanis said they would spend their free weekend time going to the movies or "dance mixers" at the then mostly male University of San Francisco, and shopping. When asked if Sandy shoplifted during those days, Tanis appeared shocked that the question was even being asked.

After a year of classes at the Catholic institution, Sandy told Ruth she was going to transfer to the newly opened University of California at Santa Barbara. Ruth, a bit disillusioned with college, decided to move back to Nevada. For the first time in eight years—excepting the brief marriage to Lee Powers—the two were apart.

Here the trail of Sante Kimes gets murky. Sante has told a court-appointed psychiatrist in 1985—who was evaluating her for a presentencing report—that she had attended UCSB for two years in the mid-1950s, studying journalism and psychology. There is no record of her ever attending the school. She has told other people that she went for four years and earned a degree. A call to the registrar's office revealed no record of Sante as a student at UCSB, even under a dozen of her aliases. There are no pictures of her in the yearbook for those years. There is no record of her even taking a single extension class, according to the school's archives.

Sandy Chambers, now in her early twenties, appeared to have given up on a college degree. She made her way back to Sacramento. Ed Chambers had retired from the military, and he and Mary had moved near California's capital where Ed had bought a small house in Rancho Cordova, a suburban village of 7,000 just outside the city. Ed, who had been promoted to Brigadier General when he retired from the military, was selling real estate part time, and Sandy stayed with them for a short while, before getting romantically involved with another Ed by the name of Edward Walker.

Eddy Walker had also been a high-school classmate of the vivacious Sandy Chambers and now the two began dating heavily, eventually marrying. Her new beau looked a lot like Lee Powers, Tanis thought. Eddy Walker became husband number two in 1956. Within a year, Sandy gave birth to her first child. Eddy named the boy Kent.

"Eddy was in construction, first with his father," Tanis told the author. "His specialty was plastering and drywall work. Sandy didn't think that was good enough, so she pushed him into becoming an architect. Sandy knew how to push and he eventually did get his architect's degree and combined it with construction. He did pretty well."

With a young son, a somewhat successful husband on the rise, and her adoptive parents nearby, one might reasonably expect the newly named Sandy Walker to now morph into the role of a happy and smug suburban housewife and mother, living happily ever after. Not a chance.

Whatever demons had pursued her since leaving the streets of Los Angeles were catching up, and had begun to nip at her heels. There were fights and accusations between Sandy and Eddy Walker, mostly about money, despite his growing success and bright future. He accused Sandy of stealing and shoplifting, confronting her about the crimes. Eddy also told friends she was schizophrenic. Sandy has a split personality, he said. Despite the baby, Eddy couldn't take the tension and gave up on the marriage. Alone, Sandy began using her original name, Sante Singhrs, again.

(Edward Walker eventually left Sacramento and returned to Carson City, where he lives today. A successful local architect, he resolutely refuses to discuss his years with either Sante or Sandy. His former wife, for that matter, described the union later as a "brother-sister arrangement," claiming he was bisexual, in spite of a child being born, a claim that is likely untrue.)

Sante Singhrs' life had sadly come full circle by the time she was in her midtwenties. She had gone through and survived two failed marriages, and given birth to a child. Pretty, almost beautiful, she could attract nearly any man with her long, jet-black locks augmented with hair pieces, along with her flashing gypsy eyes, and still-svelte figure. Sante now began to drink heavily for the first time, champagne mostly, which she didn't think really counted because, she told friends, champagne was the rich person's drink—and what she deserved from life. On February 12, 1961, Sante was arrested in Sacramento and charged with petty theft. Disgraced, she left California's capital city and returned to the streets of Los Angeles.

After the Sacramento police charges, there would be at least five criminal accusations made against Sante Singhrs or her various aliases in the 1960s. She would be arrested for grand theft in Los Angeles on December 29, 1965, and, a day later, would be accused of auto theft in the L.A. suburb of Norwalk.

"Let me tell you about the car theft," one of her former lawyers told the author, chuckling at the memory. "Sante walked into a Cadillac dealer in Norwalk and conned the salesman into letting her take a test drive in a white convertible. Alone, of course. She never came back and drove the car for months as if she owned it. When the police caught up with her, she told them she had been given the car to test drive and that's what she was doing—still test-driving it!"

Her name and aliases began appearing on several Southern California police blotters. There was a charge in Glendale in 1968 and another grand-theft charge in Riverside on November 25 of the same year. Some sources have told the author that Sante worked as a call girl in Los Angeles while Charloette Kimes's daughter, Linda, claims Sante was a prostitute in Palm Springs. However, no prostitution arrests could be found in either city and, it should be noted, there is no evidence other than the hurled accusations. Yet, if there is an inherent criminal gene in certain people as some scientists have suggested, Sante Singhrs could have been the theory's poster child.

Sante had begun to ignore her adoptive parents, the Chambers, years earlier, failing to write or call and not letting them know her whereabouts. When Mary Chambers died of cancer at the age of sixty-seven on August 7, 1969, Sante/Sandy failed to attend the funeral or the wake the day before. She didn't show up for Ed Chambers' funeral, either, when he died of emphysema on December 16, 1980. Eyebrows were raised by Carson City friends of the Chambers family.

Yet, in spite of her string of arrests, lurid background and the lack of a college degree, Sante Singhrs managed to charm her way into an important job in the late 1960s. Inexplicably, she was hired as a Washington lobbyist for a southern California managed-health-care firm, HMO Concepts. Sante was off to the nation's capital. Like so many young women who make their way to the Potomac's halls of power, she hoped to experience some of its luster, pulse, and excitement, that heretofore she had only seen on a nightly news program.

Chapter Seven

Kimes *v.* Kimes

After Charloette Kimes filed for divorce from her husband in June 1963, she began to believe that her husband was "brainwashing" their children. Their marriage of eighteen years, three months, and twenty-five days was over and, now, both her two children had quickly taken sides against her, and were assisting her husband in the courts of Orange County.

In a statement drafted on the letterhead of the powerful Los Angeles law firm that Kenneth Kimes had hired, Darling, Shattuck, Hall, and Call, sixteen-year-old Linda Kimes signed this statement, which was presented to the court on July 2nd, 1963.

> *When school starts in the fall, I will be a senior ... I am attending Mater Dei [a private Catholic coed] High School in Santa Ana, California. Since we moved to Santa Ana approximately three years ago, I have lived with my parents, first in a rented house for about six months while we were building our new home, and then moved into the completed new home at 2215 Victoria Drive ... A month and a half ago, I became aware of the fact that my mother wanted to live in a different house from my father; that my father has consistently not wanted this separation to occur, but I realized that the separation would eventually require me to be in the home of one or the other of my parents. I have given the matter careful consideration.*

My father has told me he wants me to be happy and that if I made up my mind that the way for me to be happy was to go with my mother, he would agree and would see that I was given proper support and schooling. So far as I know, my father has not changed his mind about this, but based entirely upon my own thinking, I have determined that I would like to live with my father. . . .

I have been told that my mother has filed a complaint for separate maintenance which I understand means that my mother and father will separate. I have also been told that my mother states that my father has treated her with extreme cruelty and has wrongfully inflicted upon my mother grievous mental suffering. This is not true. My father has tried to be fair to everyone in the family and my mother has been arbitrary and unreasonable with the family, not just with my father, but with me and my brother. I am also told that my mother has stated that my father nags at her and keeps her awake during all hours of the night with arguments and that he threatens to take me and my brother away from her, that he contradicts anything that my mother tells us and that by my father's words and actions, he keeps both me and my brother constantly upset. That is not the situation. All my father has tried to do is to convince my mother to remain in the home, but she insists that our home be broken up. So far as threatening to take us away from her, I have never heard my father say anything like that, but I have personally told her that I would not live with her and that I didn't believe my brother would live with her. It is not my father who keeps us upset. He has done all he could to keep from having the family broken up or having me upset. I simply cannot live with her and will do whatever I can to satisfy the Court that I should not be separated from my father.

Charloette Kimes was stung by her daughter's allegations as well as her son's almost duplicate words. Andy was fourteen when he parroted his sister's statement via his father's lawyers, except for changing the name of the school to the preppy Catholic Servite Boy's School, and adding this slightly different coda in the last paragraph.

> *My father has tried to keep the family together and so far as I have been able to see has not treated my mother unfairly or in a cruel manner. My mother has insisted that she is going to break up the home and my father is upsetting her and nagging her. My father so far as I have heard has done nothing more than try to talk matters over. I have never heard my father threaten to take me or my sister away from my mother, but he has told her that if she breaks up the home the children would have to decide which one they want to go with and he would be agreeable to doing what the children desire and that he wanted the children to be content and happy. So far as I am personally concerned I would like to be with my father. . . .*

Charloette protested the statements, adding that her husband had also plundered their joint checking account. He had removed $55,000 from it, she told the court, and transferred it to a savings account in his name only, at the Anaheim branch of the Bank of America.

She next accused her husband of trying to buy their children off. She said Ken had bought Linda a new car for her sixteenth birthday and a lavish new wardrobe. And Charloette said Ken had also put relatives in the house to spy on her.

"Both children need supervision and both are emotionally upset due to the constant battling and arguing between their parents," Charloette testified in court. Her lawyers amplified her argument further.

"Against plaintiff's wishes, defendant had his mother [Neoma Brandt Kimes] and his aunt [Alice Wardshaw] move into the house and stay for two weeks. They left for four days and then came back against [her] wishes but at the defendant's invitation. They have been in plaintiff's house until June 27, 1963. Defendant told plaintiff and the children he has had them there to 'watch her' and to look after the children, himself, and the home because plaintiff wouldn't do it. They have created more emotional upset. Defendant has told the plaintiff she is 'crazy' and he has told the children that 'she is out of her mind' many times."

Charloette also told the judge that Ken Kimes claimed she needed medical help, was "having a nervous breakdown," and should see a psychiatrist, all in front of the children. She denied that Ken didn't know her divorce action was forthcoming, and she stated he was now building what would become the Tropics Motel in Indio and that he would be away for the next four months. Then she and her attorneys went into his infidelities.

"For the past eight to nine years, defendant has gone out with other women," her lawyers wrote, accusing Ken of adultery. "Plaintiff first became aware of this four years ago. Plaintiff then begged defendant to remain home at night and to quit seeing other women. Defendant continued to go out and stay away from home. Three-and-one-half years ago plaintiff told defendant she would start separation proceedings unless he started to stay at home. [He] then promised to stay home and did so for six months. For the first three years, [Kenneth Kimes] has continued to leave home and stay away from it for one to five nights a week. The parties have discussed separation hundreds of times during the last three years and plaintiff has informed defendant on many occasions that she couldn't take his being away from home all the time. Defendant [Kenneth K. Kimes] said he could come and go as he pleased and that he 'wasn't taking orders from any woman' and that he could do as he pleased.

"Plaintiff has pleaded with the defendant to conduct his business closer to home and defendant has promised to do so. He stated that the reason he was involved with other women was because he was away from home so much.

"When the parties lived in Salinas, defendant built motels in Sacramento, Modesto, Stockton, Palo Alto, and four in Anaheim, and two in La Jolla. As soon as the parties moved to Santa Ana, the defendant started to build in Modesto and Palm Springs.

"Due to their situation, both parties have consulted with the priest in their Parish who recommended a marriage counselor. Plaintiff asked the defendant to go but defendant said, 'there is no need,' and defendant wouldn't go. The reason plaintiff left their bedroom is because defendant wouldn't let her sleep. Defendant would argue that he couldn't come home at night, that he was a wonderful provider, that she had everything she wanted and that she shouldn't be so demanding. Defendant would also continue to make personal advances [sexual overtures], although plaintiff would tell him she was too upset and she was. Defendant has used constant threats to upset the children if plaintiff didn't do as he wished.''

Charloette said in her affadavit that Ken, the defendant, was ''on a campaign to get the children'' away from her. She claimed that he had told the Kimes kids that she was overbearing, demanding, and inconsiderate and that any time she was around, he always overruled her. She again complained of Ken spoiling Linda with clothes and the new car. The inventory of family automobiles in 1965 included a 1963 Cadillac, a 1961 Cadillac, a 1961 Oldsmobile, and a 1961 Chevrolet. Their house was valued by Charloette's lawyers at ''more than'' $130,000 in 1963.

The Kimeses' divorce documents would eventually total 400 pages. It would be a two-year-long pitched battle, which set a record in Orange County for the number of court appearances for a divorce action. Reading them, one gets the general impression that Ken Kimes got what he wanted because he had the strongest lawyers. They were able to paint the picture of a hysterical housewife who had even alienated their children, at one time getting a court order to force her to take two days of mental tests. She passed, but Ken's attorneys were able to ultimately wear Charloette down with repeated legal filings, depositions, and interrogatories.

When Ken Kimes filed his first response to Charloette, he said he had no idea until six weeks before his wife took legal action, that she wanted a divorce. According to Ken, he was too busy building another new motel in Palm Springs and, because of her threats, he had commuted to and from the desert resort town, even though it was 200 miles round-trip. He said he had gone to their priest and was willing to go to counseling, but Charloette had told him "it wouldn't do any good."

Ken claimed he had tried, but Charloette was already sleeping on the sofa in the living room and insisting he sell the house, which seemed to break his heart.

"The home was built for the family and was a home for the children and I have no intention of selling it," he told the divorce court.

The Kimes patriarch said he had never threatened Charloette, and never, ever used physical violence. He denied everything his wife accused him of, and then added this topper that must have raised the eyebrows of Orange County Superior Court Judge William S. Lee:

> On numerous occasions, [Charloette] has threatened to shoot defendant, the last such occasion being approximately June 19, 1963. In addition, [Charloette] has threatened to commit suicide on numerous occasions, the last such occasion being June 21, 1963 at which time she attempted to conceal a revolver belonging to the minor daughter. [She has] on numerous occasions entered the offices of defendant and has given orders to employees and as late as July 2, 1963, she called one of the managers of the Mecca Motel and discussed the marital problems of the parties and upset the employees.

Judge Lee, forced to referee the escalating battle, decided to send the warring parties to their corners after a few rounds of the accusations, pending a final divorce decree. Literally. One of his actions was to even specify in which bedrooms Ken and Charloette could sleep.

"Both parties shall be permitted to continue to occupy the home of the parties and [Kenneth Kimes] shall have the sole and exclusive use of the upstairs guest bedroom and adjoining bath, and [Charloette Kimes] shall have the sole and exclusive use of the downstairs master bedroom and adjoining bath," he wrote.

Judge Lee also wrote an order, restraining them from discussing their marital problems in front of others, and, most pointedly, their children, forbidding them from "annoying, molesting, bothering, or threatening the other."

The jurist then warned Ken Kimes against "disposing of or hypothecating any of the community assets of the parties except in the normal course of business."

A further order demonstrated how badly matters had deteriorated in the Kimes household. Ken Kimes was ordered to give $500 each month to Charloette to be used for food and clothing. The food portion was to include Ken Kimes and the children, but the clothing allowance excluded him, thus freeing Charloette from having to replace his underwear.

Judge Lee's order lasted two weeks. Despite the separate bedrooms decree, and the order to stop fighting in front of the children, the war of nerves continued.

In mid-July 1963, the court awarded Charloette one of their three cars, the 1961 Cadillac, and raised her monthly maintenance check to $850. Judge Lee told her to clear out of the Victoria Drive house in Santa Ana by six P.M. that day, allowing her to take items of "wearing apparel, baby books, and two framed paneled baby pictures, one of each minor child" with her, despite her contention that Ken was still abusing her and attempting to get her to leave home. He also awarded her the money at Anaheim Savings and Loan to be used for Charloette's medical and legal expenses, "funds to be accounted for at the time of trial."

The judge's decision was a big win for Ken Kimes. He now had possession of the house and the children before any divorce trial took place. Charloette had asked that the judge require Ken to move out. Since she was in more physical danger than her husband, the opposite had occurred. Charloette was also ordered not to trespass on the motel properties or the corporate offices.

On September 13, 1965, Judge Lee gave Charloette her divorce, but not much more. Based on Ken's declared net worth of $1,010,000, which Charloette believed was "lowballed," she was awarded a $200,000 settlement and the 1961 Cadillac. The judgment was far from a lump sum. Out of the $200,000, Charloette was ordered to pay her attorneys

$35,000, and pay off various outstanding bills in joint accounts, ranging from Sears Roebuck to several bank installment loans. In a community property state where the split is usually fifty-fifty, what Charloette eventually got was $78,000, which the court then allowed Ken to pay off at the rate of $650 a month. It wasn't enough money to live on.

"I didn't get a stick of furniture, so I moved to Newport Beach, rented a small apartment and started all over again," Charloette told a friend. "A neighbor helped me get a job in a furniture store and in time I became its interior decorator."

Ken Kimes was awarded sole ownership of several parcels of valuable commercial land in Orange and Los Angeles counties and in Monterey and Stanislaus counties in central California. One prime piece of property, in Santa Barbara County, known as the "Wheat Ranch Development," would stay in Ken Kimes' hands for thirty years and would be the center of a controversy between Sante and members of the Kimes family after his death.

Charloette would go back into court five years later and sue Ken again. This time she charged that Ken had filed their taxes using both of their names in 1965, for the income he had earned by himself until September 13 of that year. The amount totaled $93,584.60 and she had been forced to pay taxes on it by the Internal Revenue Service. Charloette said she had been dunned $15,384 in taxes by the IRS, even though she wasn't living with her husband at any time in 1965 nor had she benefited from the money. Ken's lawyer disagreed.

"He intended to give her $200,000 gross and, except for a car, she had some small bank accounts, and some personal belongings. All of which were of no real value. This is all he intended to give her," said Ken's lawyer, adding that his client felt no responsibility for paying Charloette's share of the taxes on money he had earned but put her name on. They were, after all, still husband and wife at that time, the lawyer said.

Charloette's lawyer said it was a mistake made on "the part of [previous] counsel." She again lost—the judge ruled that she should have put that in their divorce agreement and, because she didn't, she was liable for the money.

Charloette kept her position at the furniture store and, in time, moved back to Santa Ana, purchasing a small house a few miles away from the dream home on Victoria Drive. Her children, Andy and Linda, lived with their father until they became adults. Andy followed his father into construction but worked separately from him. He lives today in Petaluma, California, and is still involved in the building industry. Linda runs an insurance agency in Orange County. Charloette, who has never remarried, in time reconciled with both of her children and says, "I have no trouble holding my head high."

PART THREE

It's not the people in prison who
worry me, it's the people who aren't.

Arthur Gore, *New York Times,* 1962

Chapter Eight

A Capital Caper

Sante Singhrs was born to be a lobbyist. After all, what is a lobbyist but a sanctioned grifter, putting the most positive spin on a client's problems and then bending the truth to sell someone else's point of view. Those who can argue convincingly for such employers are well paid. They work for an industry, move in on elected officials, and then try to con them into believing that cigarettes aren't so dangerous or that liquor doesn't need a warning label. In Sante's case, it was that medical organizations are not responsible if their employees delayed in giving surgeons the authority to operate. HMOs need to make a profit too, she said. Donating large sums to a senator's reelection campaign, wining and dining a congressman, and paying his golf fees at a pro-am tournament was something that Sante could and did do with skill and enthusiasm.

Now in her late twenties, she had grown a little chunky, and could be compared to another young Washington hopeful who would make quite a splash three decades later. It's not over the top to compare a young Sante with a Monica Lewinsky. Both came to the nation's capital to bask in its halls of power and influence. Both were Californians who had the unchecked youth and enthusiasm, with enough sultry beauty in their naturally alluring smiles—heads crowned by manes of rich, dark hair—to stop elected officials dead in their tracks. Sante used her looks to the fullest, batting her mascara-coated lashes, and cutting an impressive swath through the halls of Congress on Capitol Hill.

She would drop a name as often as she coyly lowered her eyes to vamp a legislator. Sante whispered to her jaded listeners that she was close to Katharine Graham, then the chief owner and publisher of the *Washington Post*. She told acquaintances that Kurt Waldheim, the Secretary General of the United Nations, was the godfather of her son. Others would hear that Joseph Califano, the legendary lawyer, and soon to be a part of Jimmy Carter's cabinet as his Secretary of Health, Education, and Welfare, was the godfather. Alan Cranston, the Democratic senator from California, was a former employer, she said. Paul Laxalt, the Nevada senator, would be claimed as a hometown pal. All would later deny even knowing her when contacted, though she could have worked *near* Cranston during her year with Ruth Tanis in Sacramento.

Then, there was the difficulty of Sante's acquisition of yet another new Cadillac. This time Sante and a female accomplice grifted a Cadillac Biarritz from McLean Motors in Orange County, after presenting a car salesman with a note supposedly signed by HMO Concepts President Alfred Caruso on his stationery. The letter came accompanied by a check as partial payment for the luxury automobile. The message below the letterhead effectively read, ''Send the bill for the rest of it to me.'' According to one report, Sante handed over the check in a restaurant where the salesman had delivered the car. He put it in a briefcase and then, after he left for a trip to the men's room, Sante was reported to have slipped the check back out of the briefcase, and left the restaurant with the Cadillac. Later Caruso would deny that the signature on the letter was his, implying that it was forged. No matter, Sante brazenly would say, Caruso owed her money anyway for lobbying services rendered. Soon after that, the HMO Concepts office building in Southern California had a fire, resulting in major damage. There is no record of any charges ever filed against Sante for either the fire or the alleged car scam.

How did Sante meet Kenneth K. Kimes, the romantic match surely struck up in hell? There are two versions. The first is that Sante had read a profile of Ken in an entrepreneurial magazine called *Millionaire*, liked his picture—not to mention his net worth—and set out after him during the summer of 1971. The other is that Ken Kimes went after her in 1971, when he needed a savvy Washington public-relations advisor for a new scheme he had for making money from the nation's 1976 bicentennial celebration. Actually, according to a Kimes family member, the bicentennial scam was Sante's brainstorm. Both sources do agree that the two met in Palm Springs, California, where Ken Kimes owned the Tropics motel and where Sante has an arrest record.

After Sante Singhrs came along, Ken Kimes' business style began to change. The Oklahoma hustler, who had led a life relatively free from legal actions, started getting served by a parade of process servers bearing civil suits. He fired back. Before, there had been the occasional "scraped nose in the swimming pool" lawsuit, but now a painting contractor was suing for an unpaid bill of $5000 after doing work at the Mecca motel and, instead of settling, Ken countersued. City National Bank was suing, too. With Sante around, Ken had become emboldened.

Sante behaved like a geisha around Ken Kimes. The courtesan talents she had learned at the knee of her mother, which had served her well in high school and through two marriages, now had been honed to perfection. She fussed over the middle-aged motel mogul, stirring his whiskey cocktails with her little finger, replenishing the ice in his drinks well before it was needed, and pouring a second serving of his favorite brand of bourbon while the glass was still part full. She remembered to praise his business acumen in front of others, and complimented him on his choice of ties. The new woman in his life was smart and, Kimes family sources say, also devious. One Sante trick was to drink with him from the same glass of bourbon and never swallow, spitting the spirits into a potted plant or a wastebasket while he wasn't looking, just like a hustling bar girl in a strip club who gets a commission by having men buy her booze. When he would get drunk, she would take charge. Sante told her lover she was a Catholic, despite growing up as a Presbyterian in Carson City. A spellbound Ken believed her.

"Sante asked my father what his favorite flower was. As

soon as she found out, she went to a perfume boutique and had them duplicate the scent. She wore it all the time,'' a member of the Kimes family told the author.

While not legally his trophy wife, she was at least a trophy concubine. Sante was still a beauty. She was some eighteen years younger than her vulnerable and aging fifty-six-year-old entrepreneur whose hair was getting grayer by the day. And Sante knew the type of sexual tricks that could make Ken Kimes feel like a horny teenager again. So when she came up with a scam to make money from the American Revolution Bicentennial, she let Ken believe it was all his idea.

The two grifters called the new bicentennial company "The Forum of Man," a grandiose title, considering that all they were selling were posters of old state flags and bumper stickers that extolled the 200th anniversary of the United States of America. Sante and Ken's goal was to see the posters placed on the wall of every classroom in the country. With more than 250,000 such spaces in America, a color poster selling for $10 could have given the two cash revenues of two-and-a-half million dollars. The printing cost was a mere three or four pennies per poster.

Ken Kimes thought so much of the idea that, six months after Sante proposed the plan, he incorporated the company. Sante named the enterprise Kiosk, Inc., registering the name on April 26, 1972. The headquarters of the organization was on Sky Park Circle Drive in the Orange County town of Irvine, which Ken called in news releases "our United States of America plant." He gave himself a pompous title, the "Honorary Bicentennial Ambassador of the United States of America," though he had never sought permission or approval from The American Revolution Bicentennial Commission. Sante began cranking out press statements on stationery that looked much like the official letterhead of the commission, which, by now, had been granted a command center next to the White House in Washington. Sante's first press kit contained a profile of Ken Kimes, embellishing his past and predicting future accomplishments, that was, at least, a tribute to her imagination.

Mr. Kenneth K. Kimes, Honorary Bicentennial Ambassador of the United States of the United States of America, will within the next three years plan, encourage, and develop the commemoration of our Countries [sic] 200th Birthday, and will encourage the observation and awareness of the American Bicentennial to all groups and activities throughout the Country.

Chosen from private life, Mr. Kimes does not receive any compensation for his services, and is not to be considered an official Commission employee, but serves on an Honorary basis, and has dedicated himself to the observance and success of the American Bicentennial.

Hailing from the mid-west [sic], semi retired from a career of hotel chains that became the base of his fortune and numerous philanthropies Mr. Kimes has been recognized by heads of state and the United Nations and given recognition for his contributions among the world of school children.

Within the next three years, Mr. Kimes will travel to various countries inviting Presidents and their people to participate in the American Bicentennial. He will place the gold star Bicentennial symbol pin on the world leaders in an invitation to the World to participate in the United State Bicentennial celebration. Already, Miguel Aleman, former President of Mexico, has pledged construction of the oldest church in Mexico, Guadalupe, as a Birthday gift. The Under Secretary General of the United Nations, C.V. Narasimhan, also President of the India Temple Society, has begun preliminary plans for the construction of the Taj Mahal in New York City as a Bicentennial project.

Early in May, Mr. Kimes leaves for India with the Secretary General to invite various leaders and their countries to participate in the Bicentennial of the United States . . .

Getting a full-sized replica of the Taj Mahal built in New York City may have been easier than getting the flag posters in every classroom. Sante explained to Ken that plowing through the red tape that was sure to be thrown up by thousands of school systems wasn't worth their time. What they needed, she said, was to get a charity to pay for it and then they could give them to the kids. The Rockefellers had money, and how about the Kennedys or the Ford Foundation?

In order to carry this off, Ken needed to garner some credibility. Sante got him on the program of the 1973 Rose Bowl festival to speak on the subject of patriotism and, of course, the posters. He spoke to civic groups and PTAs, grabbing a few small endorsements, preparing for his national debut.

"I'm a self-made man," he boasted. "Nobody ever gave me a dime. I used to send my money home by postal money order when I was stationed in the Aleutians [Islands]. I saved it to buy land, to develop and to build on . . ."

The patriotic fervor eventually paid off with a bonanza. Hugh Hall, the Bicentennial's acting director, allowed him to put the Bicentennial logo on his posters, and actually did proclaim him as "Honorary Ambassador," the title he was already flaunting. In a Washington ceremony, Ken was "pinned" in 1972.

"They didn't ask me for any royalties. They just thought the flags were tremendous. Mr. Hall asked if they could buy them for 'every one of our Bicentennial offices,' " Ken later told the *Washington Post*. He soon had business cards printed with his name and the title of "Honorary Bicentennial Ambassador" on them, as well as the Commission's newly designed official logo.

An embarrassed Hall would in time deny that the "pinning" ceremony was anything but a token of gratitude. He called Ken's ambassador title "self-imposed."

Sante used the pinning ceremony and the published photo of it that appeared in the *Bicentennial Times*, the Commission's newsletter, as an opportunity. Making a trip to Washington, he and Sante visited the headquarters of the U.S. Postal System, whose 37,000 post offices around the country also seemed ideal locations to sell their products.

Duke Zeller, the just-appointed public relations director

for the Bicentennial, was ready to support the odd couple. Looking back today, he said he thought them a bit strange.

"Here's this Jimmy Stewart type who says he loves his country and want to show it. And hanging on his arm is this far eastern princess who's been crossed with Auntie Mame. They were really something."

(Author's note: Observant readers will remember that Zeller's description of Sante as the flamboyant aunt in Patrick Dennis' novel of the same name is the identical appellation given to Irene Silverman by Hawaiian realtor Stuart Ho in Chapter One. Perhaps there is a good and a bad Auntie Mame.)

What Ken and Sante wanted next was nothing less than a full White House endorsement. They asked for and somehow got an audience with Patricia Nixon on April 18, 1973 (Watergate problems be damned!), to present her with the posters.

According to the White House, the memo setting up the appointment with Pat Nixon may have been forged. The giveaway evidence was the original memo supposedly sent from Richard Nixon's director of communications, Herb Klein. In the letter which asked for a date and time, was the phrase, "to kick off this noble undertaking." The same phrase was repeated verbatim by Sante in a memo confirming the appointment. Later, Herb Klein wouldn't remember writing the memo, and no carbon copy of the memo was ever found in the White House's files. Nevertheless, Sante and Ken would say they got thirty minutes with Pat Nixon. The two claimed they had a promise from her to help them place the flag posters in every schoolroom in the country. Ken soon began referring to Richard Nixon as "a close friend."

An assistant to the First Lady recalled it differently.

"It was sort of a phony thing and Mrs. Nixon realized it the very instant it happened. They tried to get Mrs. Nixon to give her blessing to their project of distributing flags in the schools. They needed a contact in Health, Education, and Welfare. Mrs. Nixon wanted nothing further to do with them."

Pat Nixon refused to release photos of her with Sante and Ken. That wasn't a problem for Sante. Ken's "public-relations counsel" just happened to have her own camera that day and captured the moment herself. She sent a photo of Pat Nixon and Ken with the flag poster in between them out to newspapers with a press release that seemed to imply endorsement of the project by the wife of the President. She would later brandish the pictures any time that her White House connections were challenged.

After the visit with Pat Nixon, Ken Kimes began claiming that he also had a document from Richard Nixon himself which named him "Honorary Ambassador." He based this on a thank-you note he had gotten from the President, a letter Richard Nixon had written after Ken had seized an opportunity to send the First Lady flowers when she was hospitalized for pneumonia later that year. The letter was addressed to "Honorary Ambassador Kenneth Kimes," a forgery that Sante and Ken had concocted jointly. He had grafted the "Honorary Ambassador" title onto Nixon's note which began, "Before another day passes, I want to thank you for the floral arrangement . . ." The two different typefaces weren't even a close match.

"If someone doesn't do what Ken is doing, the Bicentennial is going to pass us [the country] by," Sante told reporter Charlotte Hays in one of several interviews she would give on their scam. "He is a wonderful person and a dedicated American." She told Hays that Ken was a lot "more than a millionaire [to her]."

Sante revealed to the savvy social-scene writer that she and Ken were planning to host the most gala party ever given in Washington. Ken's "public-relations counsel" said that all fifty governors would be invited along with the diplomatic community. Then, perhaps with an eye on income-tax deductions, Sante told the scribe that Ken had invested "between $300,000 and $400,000" so far on his project.

"We've been invited to Washington and Mr. Hall has given us a lovely reception at his offices. It was the kind of ceremony to make you cry," she said.

Ken Kimes and Sante Singhrs had become determined to not only simply win approval by the U.S. government for

This poster was plastered throughout Irene Silverman's upper-crust New York City neighborhood within days of her disappearance.
(New York Police Department)

REWARD
$11,000

Mayor Giuliani has implemented local law 48 of 1993 and a reward of $10,000 has been posted for information leading to the whereabouts of Mrs. Irene Silverman, and the conviction of those responsible for her disappearance.

Anyone having information regarding the above vehicle (1997 dark blue/green Lincoln) or persons in the vicinity of 20 East 65th Street on or about July 4 through July 5, 1998, please contact Manhattan Detectives at (212) 694-3018. If you wish to remain anonymous, please call 1-800-577-TIPS for a reward up to $1,000.

The person in the sketch to the left is wanted for QUESTIONING. If you can provide information, please call the above numbers.

The carved godface above Mrs. Silverman's front door.
(Georgiana Havill)

Irene Silverman's five-story mansion on East 65th Street where Kenny Kimes rented a ground-floor apartment.
(Georgiana Havill)

Irene Silverman as a young ballerina, 1930.
(Lincoln Center Library for the Performing Arts)

Irene Silverman shortly before her disappearance.
(Todd Maisel/Sygma)

Sante and Ken Kimes' faux Frank Lloyd Wright house on Geronimo Way in Las Vegas, Nevada. (*Las Vegas Sun*)

The doors of the Geronimo Way house were kept locked from the inside to keep Sante's maids from escaping. (*Las Vegas Sun*)

Sante's first two husbands.
Above with Lee Powers, below with Ed Walker. (Ruth Tanis)

Kenneth K. Kimes, in
Washington, D.C.,
1974. (Star Archives)

Ken Kimes sells his Bicentennial
posters in 1973. (Star Archives)

Sante and Ken Kimes meet then-Vice President
and Mrs. Gerald Ford in 1974. (Star Archives)

Sante Kimes heads off to prison after her conviction for keeping slaves in 1986. (*Las Vegas Review Journal*)

Sante's 1986 Las Vegas mug shot. (Las Vegas Police Department)

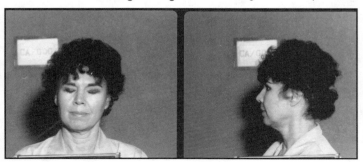

Sante/Sandy as a young horsewoman, 1951. (Ruth Tanis)

Sante/Sandy and Ruth Tanis with Kelly and Dotty Seligman, circa 1951. (Edwin Chambers)

Sante/Sandy with her first hairpiece, 1952. (Ruth Tanis)

Sante/Sandy poolside near Carson City, Nevada as a young teen. (Ruth Tanis)

David Kazdin, former Sante Kimes associate, whose body was found in a Los Angeles Dumpster in March of 1998.
(Los Angeles Police Department)

Donna Lawson, Sante's stalking horse, at her 1997 arraignment.
(Miami Police Department)

Sayed Bilal Ahmed, who disappeared in 1996 after a meeting with Sante and Kenny Kimes.
(Los Angeles Police Department)

Jose Antonio Alvarez's 1998 New York Police sketch.
(New York Police Department)

the posters, but to also insinuate themselves into the cream of Washington's society of mover and shakers. On a single night in 1974, Sante and Ken would boldly crash four A-list parties, which drew guests from the top ranks of world governments. All were supposed to have been highly secured by the hosts, but instead of that dissuading the pair, the challenge only whetted their appetite to get inside.

Ken's stirring patriotic speech at the pregame Rose Bowl festivities almost had gotten his project sanctioned by the American Revolution Bicentennial Commission. Without the knowledge of the White House, they were given the services of ARBC speechwriter Ed Stafford to help craft more of the right words for Ken to spout. Except for the decisionmakers at 1600 Pennsylvania Avenue or those at the cabinet level, the two grifters were almost there.

"We've been here five times since [the Rose Bowl speech]" Sante cooed to a Washington *Star* society columnist to drum up support. "We've been beautifully received. Those who don't call him the Ambassador call him Uncle Ken. He sends cookies to the ARBC staff at Christmas."

Sante and Ken's Washington adventures culminated on the evening of February 26, 1974, when they took a cab from their Statler-Hilton hotel to what Sante claimed later was a party at the Belgian Embassy. Ken Kimes' paramour would say she had been advised by Charles Goodspeed, the assistant head of the ARBC, to get to and attend as many embassy parties as possible while in town.

"We came to talk about a trip Mr. Kimes wants to take to Europe, paying his own way, inviting heads of state to the Bicentennial," she explained the next day in an interview, suggesting that Goodspeed had advised them that the Belgian Embassy was a good place to begin.

"I called and told them someone from the Bicentennial was coming and they said 'fine.' "

Before leaving their hotel, Sante also called an official at the offices of the Smithsonian Institution, dropped a few names, and pitched the posters to him. She later alleged that a Smithsonian executive asked her to drop off some samples at the Renwick Gallery, one of the Smithsonian's museums, which was open that evening for a party. Sante, in a typical grifter's move, would blame the evening's "mishaps" on mix-ups that weren't her fault.

"We told the cab driver to go to the Renwick Gallery, and he was foreign and looked confused," Sante explained to the Washington *Evening Star*. "So we said it was near Blair House, we thought, and that's where he dropped us off."

Moving swiftly past the Secret Service despite not having an invitation, Ken and Sante slipped into Blair House, the mansion across the street from the White House. The building was designed to serve as the home of visiting foreign leaders who stayed there as guests of the President of the United States. Ken wore a dark, pin-striped business suit, while Sante was much more attention-grabbing, dressed in a white mink turban, a flowing white chiffon dress which hid her heft, and a number of large—but fake—diamond rings on several fingers of each hand with an even larger stone glued into the center of her ear. Ken's six-foot-two height stood out among the politicians, and his long, bushy hair contrasted with the conservative short haircuts in the gathering. When asked about their party crashing, Sante acted as if she and Ken had been literally pushed through the front door.

"People were arriving for a party and we thought this was the place. So we were sort of swept inside and warmly welcomed. The Fords [Vice President of the United States Gerald and wife Betty] were wonderful people. The Vice President talked to Mr. Kimes about the Bicentennial for three or four minutes," she said.

According to several women attending the Vice President's reception, Sante was soon the center of attention. When one of the society dowagers asked her why she had a big diamond stuck in the middle of one of her ears, Sante had a ready answer.

"My father is East Indian. It's customary." Yet a few minutes later Sante told another woman she was a full-blooded American Indian.

"I don't know you," one Washington insider said to her, "and I know everyone here."

"Oh, how nice," Sante smiled back, exuding confidence, "then I have a new friend." But, when guests began to gawk and motion towards them, Sante grabbed Ken and fled Blair House.

"I was very uncomfortable and we finally asked if this was the Renwick and it wasn't," Sante recounted to a reporter later. "We were very embarrassed and left immediately. I was so nervous I developed a rash."

Not that a rash would be enough to signal an end to Sante and Ken's Pennsylvania Avenue escapades. They then walked over to the Renwick Gallery, which *was* nearly next door to Blair House, and crashed a sit-down dinner celebrating the director of the Smithsonian, Dillon Ripley, and his tenth anniversary as head of the institution. Sante claimed that, in her confusion, she left the flag posters behind at Blair House, and couldn't present them.

The dinner at the Renwick was black tie, so Ken's business suit made him stand out even further. Still, she seemed to have a wonderful memory of their brief stay with the big-money donors of the Smithsonian.

"We had a beautiful rapport at the Renwick," Sante recalled.

Meredith Johnson, the Smithsonian's curator of special collections, who was in charge of the invitation list, said he quickly asked them to leave. He had another remembrance of meeting the bizarre couple.

"I was really shook up when I saw them," Johnson said..

Sante and Ken's next move was to snare a cab and take off for the West German Embassy. Arriving at the complex, they conned their way past the embassy officials to find yet another seated dinner in progress, this one for the newly appointed American ambassador to Bulgaria. After a few minutes of small talk with the guests who were still enjoying the predinner cocktail hour, the two were approached by the wife of the German ambassador, who pointedly asked them if they were in the right place. Sante asked if she were at the Belgian Embassy. The Germans thought Sante and Ken had made an honest mistake and, since the Belgian's mansion was nearby, directed their chauffeur to take them there in one of the embassy's limousines.

Arriving at the Belgian Embassy, Ken and Sante found it dark. That didn't stop Sante from ringing the doorbell and asking about a party. The party, they were told, was at the ambassador's home. The two grifters told their newly acquired chauffeur to drive them there.

The Belgian ambassador, Andre Rahir, greeted them warmly at the door, assuming they had been invited by his wife. Ken and Sante ordered drinks and began sampling the shrimp. When the ambassador realized they were simply brazen intruders, he was very polite.

"I'm sorry, this is a private party, but you can stay for a few minutes if you like," he said to them.

Sante and Ken did stay and, after a second round of drinks, Sante boldly asked to give a speech to the guests at the function about the upcoming Bicentennial and, of course, the flag posters. Ambassador Rahir drew the line at Sante's brazen action and bounced them both. On their way out, they talked their way into a limo ride back to the Statler Hilton with the Danish Second Secretary, Christopher Bo Bramsen, and his wife.

"We knew they were gate crashers, but we also knew they couldn't get a taxi and they couldn't stay the night," said the puzzled diplomat from Denmark.

If Ken and Sante expected to get away with their night of crashing parties unscathed, they were dreaming. After Ken gave a speech to a group of disabled veterans the next night, the Washington press came down hard on them with a series of investigative stories the following morning.

THE BIGGEST CRASH SINCE 1929, headlined the *Evening Star* in a column by the arbiter of who was who among the city's elite, Betty Beale. She began, "For sheer gall, Washington has seen nothing like the pair who crashed Vice President and Mrs. Gerald Ford's diplomatic reception at Blair House, then proceeded to crash three other parties . . . [It] is the story of how far good manners, plus nerve will get you in the world of polite society, even in rank-filled Washington."

Beale seemed especially mortified that Sante and Ken had made it past the Secret Service and into the arms of the

Fords. "The Secret Service seemed unable to cope," she thundered, "offering the lame excuse that it might have been embarrassing to ask them to leave. But how much more embarrassing it would have been if one of the pair had been another Sirhan Sirhan?"

In a second story, the *Star* ran a large, unflattering head shot photo of Ken, with a particularly biting caption. Under the photo it read: "Kenneth Kimes (rhymes with 'climbs')."

The *Washington Post* assigned an investigative team to look into the background of one Kenneth K. Kimes, and soon uncovered the story of how he had forged his letter from Richard Nixon, getting White House official Robert Miller to label the document "doctored" and quoting Miller as saying, "This is not the letter that went out of the White House. Someone has obviously tampered with it."

Ken protested the charge, even to the extent of flying back to California, getting the document, and jetting back, all within seventeen hours, giving a copy of the Nixon note to a *Post* reporter. Ken seemed to believe that by simply presenting the missive, he would be vindicated. The newspaper had it examined by experts, and then magnified it, running the magnification on the front page of its *Style* section with the damning accusation ". . . the detail below indicates that the two salutations were not typed on the same machine."

Exposed, whatever goodwill Ken and Sante enjoyed with the ARBC dissolved. Ken Kimes, who had sold only 5,000 posters but had two million sitting in a warehouse, was defiant.

"I'm going to proceed with these flags in exactly the same manner as I intended. No, I won't destroy those with the Bicentennial [symbol]. I'll give them away before I do that . . .."

Ken said he would continue his speeches about the Bicentennial as well. Nothing, he said, would stop him.

"My interest is in spreading Americanism. I'm a fighter for the people. In every speech I've made I've never said one thing about the flags, only about the Bicentennial. I figured down the road there'd be some place to recoup my investment. I feel I can spend a little of my money now but

I cannot give away two million of these framed flags.''

The public disclosure of forgery by the Washington press and the reported trespassing at the Blair House reception for the Vice President instantly caught the attention of the FBI, the embarrassed Secret Service, the District of Columbia police department, and the Internal Revenue Service. FBI agents fanned out as far as California, interviewing the Kimes family and his friends. One of those visited by the FBI was Ken's daughter, now married, and living as Linda Jane Ford.

''They told my daughter in California that they thought I was misusing the title of Honorary Ambassador to promote myself. They're certainly welcome to investigate me and I'll be glad to assist them,'' Ken said.

An attorney for the Bicentennial Commission, Eugene J. Sora, quickly sent Ken a registered letter saying that his use of the Bicentennial logo on ''calling cards, flag poster displays or any such material'' was illegal, as was representing himself as an honorary ambassador.

''Willful and unauthorized use of the Bicentennial logo is an illegal act punishable by law. Unless you cease the above immediately, this matter will be submitted to the Department of Justice, for appropriate action,'' Sora threatened.

Sante shrugged off the letter. She blamed their new problems on recent changes in the officials of the Bicentennial.

''All of sudden, about a month and a half ago, they told us to come here and told us about the changes. There's been a change in the atmosphere.''

She said she'd been lectured by a Bicentennial secretary for using its office phones, who reportedly caught her talking on one of them.

''You should never use these phones. You're not a federal employee,'' the clerk chastised her.

''I don't think they're as friendly to us as they were. I think Ken is being used a little,'' his companion said.

Then, letting her guard down, Sante revealed that she was perhaps a lot more than just the public-relations advisor for Kiosk, Inc. She gushed about her feelings for Ken Kimes in one final interview with a reporter:

"Mr. Kimes has only the interests of America at heart. We're not political people. We just care about unity and getting rid of cynicism in the world. Mr. Kimes is a Will Rogers type, a self-starter, a tiger. People ask me if I'm involved with him. Well, I love him. I love his warmth."

Sante also took the opportunity to slam the ARBC.

"I'm beginning to understand why this country is so mixed up, if the commission wants to be like that. Maybe they suggested we do the wrong thing, but they could at least stand behind us."

In a final statement Ken Kimes said he was looking at the experience as a "glass is half full" kind of experience.

"This whole thing has improved my social life. Diplomats, congressmen, and all kinds of little people you've never heard of have been calling, begging me to crash their parties. I get about four invitations a night and can't accept them all. But that's okay with me, because the truth is, I don't even like cocktail parties."

Chapter Nine

A Capital Crime

Though Sante continued to be the fire that sparked the second half of Ken Kimes' life, she failed miserably at charming the children from his first marriage. Linda, his daughter, was distrustful of her from the beginning. She suspected Sante of drugging her father's favorite protein milkshake in order to lull him into an early sleep, so that she could head out for the bright lights of the city. She began to believe her father's lover was practicing what Linda called "black magic" or voodoo, going as far as to tell friends that Sante had put her in a trance at the Santa Anita racetrack, where she said she had wandered around in a daze for twenty minutes, missing a key race. She tried to stay far away from the strange relationship.

It wasn't that Ken's kids were worried about Sante getting her hands on their father's fortune. Linda's dad had let them know that the bulk of his money, now worth more than ten million dollars, would be left to her and Andy. Ken's side of the family, beginning with his mother, Neoma, and then her sister, Alice Wardshaw, soon began living with Ken and Sante at their Hawaiian home. According to Kimes family members, the elderly women had little choice: "Sante sold the house he [Ken Kimes] had built for them in Salinas right out from under them."

Life with Sante was certainly more expensive for Ken Kimes. He had been able to dominate Charloette, but now he was, in turn, was being controlled by his wily seductress. Ken had once been content to live in a single house on

Victoria Drive in Santa Ana with his family. Now there was a string of successively more expensive dwellings with Sante. There was a home in Orange County's Newport Beach, an oceanfront villa on Portlock Road in the ritzy Hawaii Kai section of Honolulu, and a house in Las Vegas. Outside the U.S., there was another beach bungalow in the Cable Beach area on the south end of New Providence Island, the population center of the Commonwealth of the Bahamas, and a condominium in Cancun, on Mexico's Caribbean coast.

Much of their time was spent in Hawaii, as far away from the Washington debacle as possible. Sante loved the sun, basking in it. Nobody had a clue to her past there yet. Ken liked Las Vegas, a haven for new-money moguls who had spent a lifetime greasing the wheels of the American economy. As a self-described ''semiretired'' business tycoon, he would spend hours popping coins into a poker machine, as long as a glass of bourbon was kept refilled by a casino maiden.

Sante had even more expensive habits. She loved walking into the most pricey restaurants in town and crudely ordering the help around.

''Gimme a drink! Gimme a menu! Gimme a telephone!'' she'd yell, her commands loaded with so many coarse expletives a sailor would have blushed.

Ken's companion liked driving costly, top-of-the-line Cadillacs and Lincolns, and seemed not to care how they were acquired as long as *she* didn't have to pay for them. Lingerie shops like Victoria's Secret rolled out the red carpet for her and Ken seemed happy to pay *that* bill. If her lover drew the line at buying her a big diamond ring, she'd buy a fake one and pretend it was real, whispering to his business friends that Ken had bought it for her.

In spite of living with a bonafide multimillionaire, Sante continued to steal, even though she wasn't always good at it. On April 26, 1972, she was arrested in Santa Ana, and charged with owning a forged credit card, as well as with grand larceny and grand theft. A few months later, on August 10, she was accused of grand theft in Palm Springs. And, on September 27, 1974, she faced yet another grand theft charge in Newport Beach. Did Ken Kimes know of her arrests?

"Of course he did. Sante was stealing for the thrill of stealing and he was into it as well. The two were made for each other," said a Kimes family member.

After the fiasco in the nation's capital, Sante had come back to Orange County and demanded they get married. Ken stayed sober enough to resist the legal ceremony. When she suspected that she couldn't get him to the altar, she began telling his friends that they were married. They had wed in Mexico, she told the family right in front of him. Ken Kimes was too intimidated to contradict her. His daughter Linda didn't believe Sante.

"On the date she said she married my father, he was sick, and my grandmother was taking care of him. He was recovering from a hair transplant. He was flat on his back and he told me he didn't marry her."

Nevertheless Sante began to use Kimes as her last name. And, even if Ken Kimes wouldn't marry, he could give her a child. On March 24, 1975, they had a boy, whom Sante named Kenneth Kareem Kimes, the first name for the father and the middle one for her brother. Gustav G. Bujkovsky, a former lawyer for the Kimeses, would call the child "perverted at birth, for a life of crime."

The bringing forth of a boy by Sante didn't soften the Kimes family's attitude towards their would-be stepmom. Linda felt that Sante was interfering in her life and, when she lost her job, she believed it was her stepmother's fault.

"All I wanted to do was have a frank talk with her," Linda said. She got a tip that Sante was in the bar of a nearby hotel in Costa Mesa, California, and drove over to confront her. Linda had inherited her mother and father's height and was a solid and imposing five-foot-eleven—more than six feet in heels. Wearing gray sweats, she swung open the door of the lounge, spotted Sante in a corner of the room, and bore down on her.

"Sante was in a booth with a man I'd never met. She had her hand in his lap and was stroking the inside of his thigh," recalled Linda.

"I said, 'Sante, I've just come to talk with you.' "

According to Linda, Sante freaked.

"She's going to kill me, she's going to kill me," Sante is reported to have yelped, fleeing from the booth, scrambling away from Linda's approach, and, with amazing agility, hurdling her stubby 160-pound body sideways over the bar itself. She cowered behind it.

Wayne Hendriks, who said he was with Sante in the bar, but denies her hand was in his lap, says Linda used obscenities when coming towards Sante.

"She [Sante] went white when she saw her." He said Linda had to be restrained and then removed by hotel security.

"That was Linda," Sante told him after the dust-up. "She hates me."

After that, relations with Linda and Sante were strained, to say the least. Linda began to see her alleged stepmother as a Svengali.

"My father became her slave. She was controlling everything."

According to sources and Sante herself, she gave birth to a second male child, called Kenian. He was born eight years after Kenny, but Sante claims she gave the infant up for adoption in Mexico. However, versions differ on the parentage of the baby. Sante had told a psychiatrist performing a mental evaluation that Ken was the father and she relinquished Kenian because "my husband was too old for a second child" and couldn't face the difficulty of having two young kids running through the house. Linda and other Kimes family members flatly dispute the tale and label her story ludicrous.

"My father loved children. The baby was not his. It came from another man."

Mexico had become a favorite playground for Ken and Sante in the 1970s. Both spoke passable Spanish, and sources describe Sante as one who enjoyed roaming the slums of Mexico City, finding poor teenage girls, and offering them jobs as servants in one of her several homes. The discovery of a young girl roaming the streets was nearly identical to the way Mary and Ed Chambers had found her some twenty-five years earlier. And, though Sante would tell the girls they would be taken care of and well paid in America, she did the opposite. When Sante got them back to the United States—they were imported illegally—she began to keep them in a state of involuntary servitude or slavery. There is no other word to describe it. The girls received no salary, and were forced to work seven days a week from five in the morning until midnight. Most were illiterate and spoke no English. Sante taught them to fear her by beating and threatening them. To quit was to escape from behind the high, closed walls of Sante and Ken's estates, and that was difficult.

Sante also became a *coyote* for some Mexican women she found. In the parlance of the U.S. Immigration and Naturalization Service, that means someone who guides illegal immigrants into the U.S. for money. Sources have told the author that for a fee of $1500, Sante would transport a young woman to the border, con a border guard into believing she was a household servant, then abandon her somewhere in California to fend for herself.

Though Ken and Sante had many homes in warm climes, they couldn't, it seems, stay away from the nation's capital. Perhaps they wished to extract a perverse revenge for the embarrassment they had suffered in Washington. How else to explain Ken and Sante being charged jointly with stealing a dark mink coat worth $10,000 and, for Ken separately, a dark wool overcoat worth $200?

According to witnesses, court reports and newspaper accounts, Ken and Sante moved from hotel to hotel in the first week of February 1980 looking for a big criminal score. On February 3, Sante and Ken lifted an overcoat from a man by the name of John F. Booth. The businessman had left it unguarded at an inn a few blocks away from the Mayflower, the luxury Washington, D.C., hotel on Connecticut Avenue, where the two were staying with an entourage of servants. Kenny, now nearly five, was tended to by a nanny, Sante had a personal maid with her, one of her "Mexican discoveries" as she sometimes referred to them, and Ken had a "Man Friday," the name he used for his personal servant.

While most people that wealthy might have spent their free time playing tennis or visiting the museums, Sante and Ken spent their days and nights pursuing a more dangerous game—stealing for the thrill of it.

The next evening, which hit nineteen degrees and was described as "the coldest night of the year" by one newspaper, the two grifters made their big heist—the $10,000 mink coat. Sante and Ken lifted it from a woman who happened to look away at the wrong time. Brazen as can be, the two stole it from the piano bar lounge at the Mayflower, a few floors below the small suite in which they were staying. The name of the lounge was the "Town and Country," coincidentally, the name of one of multimillionaire Ken's group of motels. They did it together, using hand signals and looks. Sante took the coat, while Ken acted as her lookout.

It was amazing the way it went down. Charles Crane, a Hewlett Packard executive from California, was visiting Washington that day, as was Rena Cusma, an administrator for the state of Oregon. The two had discovered each other and were chatting over drinks. At the next table of the lounge was a married couple, Robert and Katherine Ann Kenworthy, with some of their friends. Mrs. Kenworthy dropped her dark mink coat over the chair behind her. Ken and Sante, who were also in the lounge, noticed the woman's inattention to the luxurious item. But people had already paid attention to Sante. Earlier, those drinking in the bar had exclaimed over her resemblance to Elizabeth Taylor. Rena Beachy was one of those in the hotel that night who noticed the lookalike.

"She had clearly made herself up to look like her. She was imitating Elizabeth Taylor. It was a striking resemblance," Beachy recalled.

It was Crane who first observed Ken and Sante changing tables in order to sit just behind the Kenworthys. He watched Sante take the Kenworthy mink from the chair, calmly put it on, and then appeared to absentmindedly put her own white one on over the top of Kenworthy's coat, covering it up. During Sante's actions, Crane's mouth flew open and he nudged his newly discovered companion to watch the silent drama that was taking place right in front of them. Sante, wearing the two coats, left the lounge with Ken, and returned a few minutes later without either coat. At that point, witnesses would remember Sante going up to the Kenworthy couple and striking up a conversation as if nothing had happened, then leaving the lounge. A few minutes later the Kenworthy couple discovered that her mink was gone and they became upset, loudly summoning the hotel security staff. Charles Crane and his companion described what had happened, saying that they had seen the woman steal the coat but hadn't told the Kenworthys instantly because, as the Californian told the hotel cops, "We could not believe what had happened had really happened."

Rena Beachy had much the same reaction. She talked to herself.

"I said, 'Did I really see that?' "

The District of Columbia police were called and, with Beachy's, Crane's, and Cusma's "fat Liz Taylor" description, Sante's seventh floor junior suite was quickly located. Inside the rooms, the police were unable to find the stolen mink coat—just John Booth's expensive wool overcoat. There were several other mink coats that, curiously, had had their labels and linings removed crudely with scissors. That made identifying the true owner of the coats impossible. A detective then noticed that one of the windows was not quite shut against the chill night air. Opening it all the way, he looked out and saw the satin lining of a coat—which turned out to be Mrs. Kenworthy's—balled up and thrown down to the landing below. The $10,000 Kenworthy mink itself would be found by a hotel maid several days later, stashed behind an ice machine near Sante's room. Ken and Sante were arrested and both spent the night in the city jail. The next day, the two appeared before D.C. Judge Sheila Bowers, with a hastily acquired attorney, Bill Burleson, who had been procured by Ken's "Man Friday." They asked to be released without bail since it was "all a mistake."

The judge said she couldn't do that since they didn't have a Washington address. Oh, but we do, said Sante, it's 1127 Connecticut Avenue. The judge had to explain that giving the address of the Mayflower Hotel where they had stayed for just two nights did not qualify them for a local residency. Ken's "Man Friday" then asked to speak, introducing himself as "Mr. Kimes' butler." He told the judge under oath that Ken was worth $12 million. Ken next dropped the name of an undersecretary of the United Nations who, he said, would vouch for them, and then claimed to have an important meeting scheduled with President Jimmy Carter for the following day. Seemingly overwhelmed by the verbal barrage, Judge Bowers allowed them to post a $4000 bond as bail—which a local bonding company underwrote, billing Ken the standard ten percent, or $400, as a fee. Both Sante and Ken were charged jointly with one count of petty larceny for the man's overcoat and one count of grand larceny for the mink.

On the arrest form, Sante let the police spell her name phonetically as Shante, and lowered her age by a dozen years, by giving them the inaccurate birth date of July 24, 1946. In spite of having several homes, Sante and Ken listed their residence in California as 1544 South Harbor Boulevard, which was the address of the Mecca Motel.

Out of jail and back at her hotel, Sante insisted on giving the Washington press corps a blow-by-blow account of her ordeal. The *Washington Post* published her complaint along with an unflattering description of their earlier escapades. Phrases describing them as the "Washington party-crashers" and Ken as the millionaire who "tried to pass himself off as Honorary Ambassador" couldn't have pleased the couple. The newspaper—which had checked—also pointed out that Ken's "appointment" with President Carter was actually an upgraded tour of the White House, arranged through a member of Congress. It headlined their story "Minky Business." In one interview, Sante behaved as if she had never seen the inside of a precinct holding cell before.

"It was awful," Sante claimed, wearing a pair of gaudy rhinestone-rimmed glasses at a hastily organized interview in the lobby of the Mayflower. "They handcuffed us, frisked us, and then put us in these little green-barred closets that had a toilet with no seat!

"The police forced their way into my room at two in the

morning. I had been asleep, I was stark naked and they pushed me around and started searching all over the room. I said we knew nothing. They took us and my remaining furs down to the station.''

Sante said the cops had injured her wrists in handcuffing her. She threatened a lawsuit.

Mrs Kimes used the words ''remaining furs'' because her version of what happened differed greatly from the police account. In fact, she turned the story on its ear.

''It was my coat that was stolen.'' was Sante's version. (The *Post* also spelled her name as Shante in its story.) The millionaire's ''wife'' claimed she had checked her own brown mink at the hotel's Carvery Restaurant and then, somehow, had forgotten to pick it up. She said when she did go to get it, the manager brought out a mink that Sante sniffed was ''not nearly the quality of my own.'' Then Mrs. Kimes told reporters she had gone to the police station to file a missing fur-coat report for insurance reasons. After deflecting other questions concerning the coat theft, Sante seemed to explode.

''It's an outrage! To think that I would need to steal someone's fur!''

Getting Sante and Ken to a jury trial was much easier to schedule for the Superior Court of the District of Columbia than to see their court date become a reality. The trial of Kenneth K. Kimes was scheduled for August 11 the same year but in July, his attorney, Robert P. Watkins, of Williams and Connolly, the famed criminal law firm, sent a letter to the court, claiming that Ken had a long history of ''hypertensive vascular disease, peripheral vascular insufficiency, and cerebrovascular insufficiency with transient ischemic attacks.'' He enclosed a doctor's affidavit to buttress his claim.

''The defendant is recuperating from these diseases in Hawaii and is too ill to travel to Washington, D.C. for a trial on August 11, 1980,'' Watkins wrote. The lawyer claimed that Ken was all but at death's door.

''The life and health of the defendant will be endangered if he is forced to travel from Hawaii to the District of Co-

lumbia to undergo the ordeal of a trial at the present time
. . . the defendant's condition has limited counsel's ability to
communicate with him and to prepare his defense.''

Bob Watkins said he expected his client's condition to
improve in the next few months. But, after getting the continuance, the millionaire motel mogul also got lucky. John
Booth, the owner of the purloined overcoat, died, and Watkins got the charges against Ken dropped. That left Sante
still facing a grand larceny rap. The District of Columbia
courts were still determined to try his wife. Mrs Kimes, for
her part, was equally determined not to set foot in a D.C.
court ever again.

After three more years of continuances, a trial was finally
scheduled for April 16, 1984. Just before that date, Sante
sent in a notarized letter from a Hawaiian doctor, a G. P.
Pares, M.D., to say that Sante had surgery scheduled for
that very same day. To the untrained eye, the signature on
the document (the doctor did not use a letterhead) looked a
lot like the handwriting that Sante had used in signing her
name and address to the original charges. In fact, with its
misspellings and poor grammar, one could easily come to
the conclusion that Sante had written it herself:

> The patient, Sante Kimes, is in the process to be
> sceduled [sic] for surgery on an emergency basis be-
> cause of unpredictable crisis; present is abdominal
> distention secondary to ovarian cyst and abdominal
> tumor. Pelvic sonogram has revealed acute pancrea-
> titis, [sic] cystocele, and rectocele.
>
> The patient is scheduled for surgery the week after
> April 16, 1984. Any delay for the surgery could cost
> the patient's life as we no longer continue on medical
> regime resulting from the Court appointed date of
> April 16, 1984. She is attempting to resolve court ac-
> tion to sustain her permanently ill husband and their
> small son.
>
> In conclusion, clinical condition is critical. Any
> stress is detrimental for the above mentioned plan,
> mainly surgery, and other.

The D.C. Superior Court gave Sante still another six-month extension. In November of that year, the court got another letter, this time from a doctor in Mexico City, who happened to use some phrases very similar to those the doctor in Hawaii did when giving Sante her original excuse, despite the difference in nationalities:

> *Sante Kimes has been scheduled for surgery emergency basis: there is present abdominal distention, secondary to cyst and abdominal tumor with sonogram revealing pancreatitis and rectocele. Generalized edema is present.*
>
> *On November 9, 1984 while in Washington, D.C., attempting to resolve court action, abdominal distention became so severe the patient was taken to see Dr. Helen Capone, Southern Maryland Hospital and was advised to remain there for medical assistance. Because of extreme anxiety in long illness, Mrs. Kimes insisted on leaving that facility to return home to receive medical treatment, rather than be treated by new physicians.*
>
> *The patient is in critical condition. Medical complications must be resoved [sic] prior to operative surgery. She is not able conduct any physical activities: physical agitations are hazardous and must be avoided to prevent possible rupture of the pancreas.*
>
> *Clinical condition is critical and at this time I cannot state when operative surgery is possible . . .*

Sante was finally brought into court in July 1985, more than five years after D.C. police filed their charges. Her trial took six days. The legal show served as cheap entertainment for the more jaded court goers, whose hobby was to seek out such courthouse circuses.

By now, Sante had hired and fired most of the better criminal attorneys in Washington. Still, during her trial, she had the services of two of the best lawyers in the city—Gary Kohlman and Joel Klein. Kohlman believed that the more men he could get on the jury, the more sympathy Sante would get. Prosecutor Ken Carroll, sensing Kohlman's ploy, vetoed as many males as he could. Kohlman's biggest triumph was getting the coat's value reduced from $10,000 to $6500.

Sante Kimes appeared in court each day as if she were back in high school, starring in the senior class play. Her costumes were attention-getting flowing white-and-pink gowns, more suitable for a gala evening at a theater's first night than a day in court. Witnesses made several unflattering references to her as they mounted the stand and compared Sante to her favorite film star. She was called "a fatter Elizabeth Taylor" by one witness and a "bad Liz" by another, expressions that drew a Dragon Lady scowl. Sante never took the stand herself, preferring to make her grand entrances and exits each day as if she was an aging silent-screen star walking towards the camera for a close-up.

On the morning of July 18, the twelve-person jury began deliberating. By two-thirty in the afternoon it had reached a decision. However, the judge soon discovered he had a problem. Sante had disappeared and nobody, not even her lawyer, had any idea where she could be found. The puzzled justice granted an hour's stay for announcing the judgment, but Sante failed to materialize. Gary Kohlman then asked for a day's delay in the decision but the judge was anxious to release the jury—who had been on duty for weeks—and let them go home. He allowed them to give their verdict. It was guilty as charged—what most courthouse observers had expected. The judge then issued a bench warrant for Sante, approving her arrest and revoking the bail bond.

Gary Kohlman eventually heard from Sante three days later by a telegram sent from California. She had a story to tell everyone. It was a grand, tall tale, and it must have stretched the faith of even the most gullible of defense attorneys.

"I went out for lunch, began walking across a street, and was hit by a large van," the essence of her fable began. "I wound up in the emergency room of the Arlington [Virginia] Hospital and in the confusion my purse and identification was stolen so they don't have a record of my being there and anyway, they released me after a few hours because I didn't have a concussion." [She later claimed she did.] "I immediately flew home to California to get further attention from my own medical doctors. Oh, and by the way, how's my case going?"

"It seemed an appropriate ending," said Gary Kohlman at the time. "It was the last play."

In retrospect, it may have been the beginning. Sante got new lawyers and appealed. She would soon make what the legal profession calls "case law."

Some three years later, the District of Columbia's Court of Appeals overturned the verdict on a technicality. "A criminal defendant's right to be present at the return of a jury verdict implicates the right of due process under the Fifth Amendment," the decision began.

In plain English, because Sante had slipped out before the verdict was read, she walked free. To quote the court further, her "absence from the trial was involuntary and her constitutional right to be present was at issue. The Court of Appeals will reverse a conviction unless the Government proves the defendant's absence was harmless beyond a reasonable doubt. The trial court's failure to conduct, either at trial or at sentencing, an inquiry into the circumstances surrounding defendant's absence from trial was error, requiring remand for necessary finding as to voluntariness, where counsel for defendant objected at trial to court's proceeding to verdict when defendant was not present."

Sante's eventual not-guilty verdict by the liberal D.C. Court of Appeals was a stroke of good fortune. But her luck had run out long before the reversal in the nation's capital on October 31, 1989. Less than three weeks after returning to California from allegedly being run over by an automobile on the day of the mink coat theft verdict, she and Ken were arrested again.

This time the FBI did the honors. The charge was keeping slaves.

Chapter Ten

The Boy Slave

Imagine, for a moment, you are Kenneth Kareem Kimes as a small child, the son of Kenneth Keith Kimes and Sante Louise Kimes. You have a mother and a father who are older than most kids' grandparents. Your dad is eligible for Social Security and your mother is trying to turn back time by exploring every plastic surgery procedure available, in one last attempt to preserve her looks. As appendages in this geriatric drama are the walking dead. Your dad's mom and aunt have also become a part of the Kimes household, allied with him, and an enemy of your mother. Then, sometimes, there's Kent Walker, your half-brother, wandering around, heading for the refrigerator for food. In this seamy saga, which is more lurid than any day with *The Addams Family*, you learn to watch your back from all your mother's visitors. You feel Kent will want his share of the inheritance someday, so you learn to look out for yourself early.

Each day, as a small child—and you can't miss it—your mother is yelling and screaming at the non-English-speaking household help. Sometimes she beats them with a wooden coathanger, at other times pours scalding water over exposed skin, and maybe she puts a hot iron to their backsides. It's impossible to block out hearing their loud cries, or their softly sobbing alone in their rooms. These young women are your allies most of the time, watching you, feeding you. They are your chief companions. Lacking real brothers or sisters, you live isolated, in a series of neglected mansions, so that it's impossible to have more than a few outside friends, and those you do have are approved by your mother first. She arbitrarily holds veto power over each playmate, usually choosing them for you. Your mother sits in judgment of each child's looks and, particularly, their station in life. Few are good enough. Your dad copes by drinking himself into a stupor each day, withdrawing into what one business associate would call "a miniature Howard Hughes persona." His "ambassador" scheme has gone awry, and his plans of importance with it. He's just another run-of-the-mill rich guy, with a criminal record to boot.

When you are two years old, your mom and dad are suspected of setting fire to one of their own hotels, the Times Square on Flamingo Road, in order to get insurance money. Before the fire is out, the fire department's spokesman, Gary Hunt, is talking about "suspicion of arson."

When you are still four, and sleeping in a hotel in Washington near your mother, a police posse bangs on the door in the middle of the night and arrests both your mom and dad. The cops spirit them away for twenty-four hours and put them in a cooler with bars.

Now you are six, and the neighbors' children are off to school, but your own mom won't let you go, instead providing you with a revolving band of tutors to teach you the ABCs. What did one of those impudent private teachers call you, "a bad mama's boy"?

And then it gets worse.

"His mother was his role model. They spent all their time together. Kenny didn't get enough exposure to other people and other families to know what was normal and what wasn't," another tutor will later tell the press.

As soon as you can read, Mom shows you her secret album. She calls it the "rainbow book" but it might as well be called the "people I want dead" register. Your mother has cut out pictures and newspaper clippings of men and women she says are her enemies. Mom believes that by staring at the photos she can do harm to these folks. You try to help mama along, by staring at her enemies list right along with her. When you're a man, the New York cops will find one of the books in your mother's Lincoln. But now, the neighborhood is shunning your family and calling you ''the devil's spawn''—behind your back, but you probably hear their words anyway. Rumors spread that your mom is not to be trusted. After a visit from her, the folks next door notice that their watches and rings are missing.

By the time you are ten, you're willing to be what an FBI agent later describes as ''the guard dog for the maids. They were all afraid of [Kenny],'' the FBI's Tom Nicodemus says.

It's not easy growing up as Kenny Kimes. When you become old enough to ride a two-wheeled bike, you are more familiar with insurance investigators, wandering around your home and snooping, than with the gardener who mows the lawn. It's your mom's new occupation. She tries to satisfy the insurance-claim adjustors' increasingly pointed questions. They are suspicious. But, that's where the big payoffs are, she's decided. Your dad doesn't fault Sante for her new passion—collecting thousands of dollars for losses because of fires and theft—he thinks it's easy money. Not that she has given up the petty thefts, the grifts, the fun stuff. She still relishes disguising herself as a little old lady to get sympathy from shopkeepers, and perhaps grab a $100 antique for twenty bucks.

Nobody is beyond the grifting talents of your mom. She hires the homeless to mow the lawn, then drives them back across town and ''sadistic as all get-out,'' as a former lawyer describes her, hands them an envelope that she says has two twenty-dollar bills inside. As she drives away, the poor unfortunates find out the envelope's empty. Mama also loves lifting a Cadillac now and then, usually protecting herself by parking it in a nearby driveway. One time, Mom grabs a Caddy and cons a neighbor, Pat Christopher, who happens to be the wife of Grant Christopherson, a former FBI agent and the chief investigator for the State Bar of California. The investigator's spouse lets Mom leave the stolen car parked in her driveway off and on for two months. Soon afterward, your mother steals the investigator's stationery. That could come in handy later on.

It's her way of life and you have been sucked into this poisoned maelstrom at birth. Your first time in trouble is when you burn down a neighbor's house in Las Vegas as a youngster, with a Fourth of July rocket. It causes $170,000 in damages. Mom settles with them for pennies on the dollar. When you want one of those fancy new laptops, your mother gets you one by filing the insurance claim for the ''stolen'' electronic gadget even before she buys the computer. The garage in your house is stuffed with television sets and other appliances that appear there mysteriously in the middle of the night. Your mom, and your dad too, see conquests and thrills in these scams and illegal endeavors. Living with your parents is always a little taste of life on the lam and, more often, a life that is way over the legal line. She will give you any material possession you desire as long as you obey her. You learn to play the game.

As a teen you watch your mom and dad impersonate the elderly owners of a Las Vegas house a few doors down from Wayne Newton. It's a foreshadowing of the Irene Silverman affair. Lawsuits fly back and forth and the old couple say your parents have used their checks to withdraw $7,000 from their account.

''We were able to extricate ourselves from their clutches,'' a relieved Paul Richards, the master of the house, later tells the New York *Daily News*.

And you live in Las Vegas! The grifting capital of the world. The home of mobsters and the hideout of hitmen for decades. Was there a better place to learn your trade?

When you get through adolescence, and start to get interested in girls, they have to go through your mother first. You are a handsome teen, but when you express an interest your mom says they're all ''tramps.'' She wants you interested in her, not them. You're conflicted. The sexual urge inside doesn't know in which direction to channel your most basic desires.

''Sante was a very domineering person. I would hate to imagine what it would be like to have her as a mother. That kid didn't stand a chance,'' former attorney Doug Crawford concludes.

It was not easy being her boy slave, was it, Kenny Kimes?

*　　*　　*

While Kenny was still five, his mother filed an insurance claim on an "antique tapestry quilt," that she said had been stolen from their oceanfront home in Hawaii. An investigator from the insurance firm, Sequoia National, soon arrived to check out Sante's claim, which she had filed claiming it was worth more than $100,000, according to family sources.

When Ken's elderly aunt, Alice Wardshaw, was questioned, she told the investigator that she didn't remember ever seeing such a tapestry in the home. Sante went to court to assert her claim, and not only lost, but was assessed a penalty and court costs.

"She was furious that Alice had let her down," said a family source. "She kept her locked in a room and starved her."

Sante's "husband," his family members claim, did nothing to discourage the mistreatment. Hearing of her wrath, Kimes family members flew to Hawaii in a rescue attempt. Scooping Alice up, they brought her back to the mainland to be put into an Orange County nursing home, a move, they say, turned out to be too late.

"When she was admitted, the doctors gave her a physical examination. They discovered that part of her vagina had been sewn up with black thread," said a Kimes family member, adding that the family believes the home surgery was part of Sante's "black magic" practices.

Kenneth Kimes' aunt died shortly thereafter and, when family members arrived at the mortuary to ask for an autopsy before burial, they discovered that Sante and Ken Kimes had been there first. Alice Wardshaw had been ordered cremated. To this day, they believe that Sante is responsible for her death.

With the witness who had testified against her now dead, Sante hired another lawyer, Charles Catterlin, to appeal the decision. Catterlin still rues the day he ever laid eyes on Sante Kimes.

"I basically got stiffed," Catterlin recalled from his retirement residence in in the Gulf Coast town of Harlingen, Texas.

"She conned me into flying out to Hawaii from California, telling me to put the flight on my credit card and she'd reimburse me when I got there. Of course, I never even got *that* money. She conned the pants off me.''

Catterlin remembered Sante doing much of the talking, her conversation peppered with obscenities. He thought Sante's husband was reclusive. Sante said he was sick. His most distinct memory was the diamond ring on her hand, which he estimated to be at least five carats. On second glance, he decided it was fake.

"But," he recalled, still with awe in his voice, "it was a magnificient oceanfront home.''

Sante lost the appeal on the tapestry. Neither one of the Kimeses ever paid Catterlin one dollar for his services.

"I'd call their house and ask to speak with Mr. Kimes about the debt. Sante would say he was sick and couldn't come to the phone. He was hiding from me." On June 5, 1981, an angry Catterlin sued Sante and Ken for $12,000 in legal fees, serving them with the lawsuit at the Mecca Motel in Anaheim. Of interest is how he addressed the two, "Kenneth K. Kimes, et al." He enclosed an attachment, spelling out the defendants as:

> Kenneth K. Kimes and Mrs. Kenneth K. Kimes, aka Sante Kimes, aka Sante Singres Kimes, aka Sandy Kimes, aka Sandra Louise Walker, aka Louise Sante Walker, aka Santee Louise Walker, aka Marjorie Walker, aka Mrs. Ed Walker, aka Sandy Walker, aka Louise Walker, aka Sandra Louise Chambers, aka Sandy Chambers, aka Sante Louisa Chambers, aka Sante Louisa Powers, aka Sandra L. Singhers, aka Sane Taj Singhrs, aka Sante Saligmen, aka Sandy Jacobson, aka Sandra Singer.

Catterlin may have believed he had all his bases covered by listing the aliases. Actually, he was probably using less than half of the combinations of the names used by the woman calling herself Mrs. Kenneth K. Kimes.

Vittorio Raho says that he was Kenny's "first real friend." Raho, now a medical student, remembers living next door to Kenny in Las Vegas in the 1980s. Kenny was a wonderful companion, who shared his toys and used his family's money to buy friendship, paying for their movie tickets and meals at McDonald's.

Vittorio's dad, Benito, thought Kenny's mom Sante looked a lot like the movie actress too.

"She dressed in white all of the time. With her hair and the makeup she did look a lot like Elizabeth Taylor, to tell the truth," he said.

Benito also recalled maids trying to run away from the Kimeses Las Vegas house, screaming for help. He thought that was a bit strange. He also recalled a cruel, condescending Sante Kimes, anxious to put him and others in their places.

"She told me her son was a genius and mine wasn't, and she didn't want them together."

Sandra Raho also recalls the maids being kept barefoot next door.

"She was a queen over there. The girls did her bidding."

But the Raho family loved Kenny, not Sante, and they judged his father as harmless. So they took pains to invite him to kick a soccer ball around with the neighborhood children on a dead-end street. For a few minutes, Kenny was an ordinary boy, appearing to be like the other fifth and sixth graders.

"He was a normal kid, very shy," Benito said. His son also defended him.

'There was no impulse in Kenny to cheat or lie."

A second Las Vegas neighbor, who didn't want to be identified because of possible retribution, said, "You just knew she [Sante] was strange. The moment you spoke to her, you just didn't want your child to be in her company. When Kenny was little she didn't want anyone playing with him."

Another friend, this time from his Hawaii days, claims she was Kenny's "hired playmate."

"I was his only friend," Kara Craver-Jones told the *New York Post*. I was the hired playmate, I guess.

"We had an intense relationship. He was kind of a dork,

he lacked social skills, but he was really nice. He wasn't evil or scary to me then.''

Kara said it wasn't too long before Sante began ordering the two of them around.

''He wasn't allowed to have any other friends. We had to do what his mom said and when she said it. He never talked back. She was dominant of him, of me, of everybody. I just thought that's the way their life was supposed to be like.''

Kara's mom, Denise, recalls, ''Sante was a demanding, domineering woman. She was on stage all the time.''

They agree that Kenny was a sad case because of his mother.

''He was really lonely,'' said Kara. ''When we were alone, he told me he wished he could live more of the life I had.''

Kara said that Sante trotted out an old gambit during her friendship with Kenny. Sante promised she would send them both to Russia as ''youth ambassadors.''

Still Kara recalls being a bit puzzled by Sante's flash on one hand and the lack of cash on the other. It was to her as if the Kimes family wanted material possessions without ever paying for them. She was transported each day to Kenny's house in a limousine, but she remembers never seeing them paying for anything.

''I never saw a single dollar. They'd send us to the store, but the stuff would go on a tab. We'd go to Louis Vuitton or Gucci and Kenny would [choose an item] and say he'd come back to get it. He never did.''

On her birthday, Kenny gave her a cheap tee-shirt. Kenny then began to talk to her, cryptically, about the family's troubles.

'' 'We have Mafia troubles and I can't tell you this,' Kenny would say, or 'We have troubles in Santa Monica, but I can't talk to you about it,' '' Kenny would tell her.

It was hard to confide in her, Kara recalled. Sante was always around, usually within earshot.

''I thought he was a lonely boy, because he was an only child in a wealthy family. But there were these scared little blurts and stops coming from him.''

Once Kara got a glimpse of Sante's many wigs on stands in a bedroom. Kenny said she had just undergone chemotherapy. The boy slave was learning the scams—make a statement to win sympathy and unbalance the mark. It's a learned reflex among grifters. And, in the end, Sante managed to scam Kara and her mom not once, but twice.

The first was when Sante told them she would like to buy their motorized raft, which was up for sale. Sante took it for a week, damaged it, ran the gas to empty, and never paid a nickel.

The second was when Sante learned that Denise made a living from creating original glass artwork. She offered to help them sell and promote the pieces. She took several to display in her house.

"Every time we'd ask about the glass she said she would give us the money when she sold some or 'when I decide.' There was always an excuse."

Denise said they never got paid or were ever given the artwork back. The relationship ended when the Kimeses' Hawaiian house burned down. It was the second time the Hawaiian house of Ken and Sante had been in a fire (the first time had been in 1978), but the mother and daughter never knew that. According to her former lawyer, Gus Bujkovsky, Sante blamed the second fire on attorney David C. Schutter. Ken's lover claimed Schutter worked for the "Hawaiian Mafia" or alternately the "Hawaiian Crime Syndicate." Sante said he was her neighbor and mistreated his maids. Sante told everyone who would listen that the "mobster lawyer" didn't like her much and had it in for her. In truth, David C. Schutter may not have liked her. The Honolulu attorney would represent her Latino maids in their successful 1980s civil suit against Sante and her insurance company, deposing her time after time in prison.

Another Hawaiian neighbor, Elayne Geller, remembers a seven-year-old Kenny watching her in a bar, while she and Sante negotiated for her to housesit the mansion. Geller soon found out she was also expected to guard a Mexican maid. She was told the servant began work Monday mornings and continued through Sunday night. In an interview with Michael Daly of the *Daily News*, Geller told of her meeting with the Kimes family.

"I don't understand. Doesn't she get a day off?" Geller said she asked Sante Kimes.

"No."

"What if she gets sick?"

"Give her an aspirin."

"What if she gets very sick?"

"She is not to go out or [use the telephone]."

She remembered trying to make small talk with Kenny and Papa Kimes and being cut off by Sante. The boy and his dad stayed mute.

"They were to keep their mouths shut while she did the talking. Everyone stood in her shade," said Geller.

But life with Sante was about to take a turn for the better for young Kenny Kimes. His mom's luck had finally run out, and she was to be sent off for some hard time in a Federal Correctional Institute for women. Boyhood buddy Vittorio Raho would call this phase in his friend's life "Kenny's golden years."

Chapter Eleven

The Slave Girls

The second date Sante claimed she married Ken Kimes was, Monday, April 5, 1981, in Las Vegas. A marriage certificate (*see* Exhibit A) obtained by the author shows that the ceremony took place at the "World Famous Chapel of the Bells" on Las Vegas Boulevard, and was witnessed by Michael S. Rose and performed by the Reverend Albert Alalouf.

Members of the Kimes family believe that the certificate is fraudulent, and that Sante either showed up with an impostor or that the signature is forged. Authorities in Clark County, Nevada, where Las Vegas is located, say that the certificate may or may not be accurate. Of interest is the fact that the certificate was recorded more than a month later, on May 8, 1981. Most municipalities in the U.S. insist on a marriage being recorded within five days of the event.

Certainly, one has to wonder why Sante has claimed two wedding dates and why both she and Ken waited more than six years after their son Kenny was born to legalize their union. Finally, given Sante's flamboyance, it's hard to understand why she would choose a Monday and a legendary Las Vegas quickie marriage mill with a witness who no doubt worked for the wedding factory to legalize their relationship.

By midsummer 1985, several of Sante's slave girls had escaped from her homes, bearing wild tales. Their stories had aroused the interest of law-enforcement agencies within the federal government.

In July that year, one of her captives, Amalia Osorio, climbed over a wall in Las Vegas and ran to a nearby house.

"She looked panicky, frantic," the Kimeses' neighbor recalled. The young woman, in tears, and speaking broken English, asked her to call the police.

In Hawaii, one of Sante's Mexican maids had begged another neighbor, Beverly Stone, to aid her in an escape. Stone had once helped to transport a maid from Los Angeles to Hawaii for Sante. Now, after hearing the girl's story of being locked in a motor home, she was more than willing to see that the servant got back to the mainland.

"She said she had never been paid, that she was like a slave, that she'd been burned and threatened," Stone told police.

In wealthy La Jolla, California, Sante and Ken had leased a lavish three-bedroom condominium, at the corner of Via Mallorca and Caminito Ameca, from a couple they had met in Calexico, the scruffy border town at the southern tip of the Imperial Valley. It was in La Jolla that one of Sante's servant's tales finally got the attention of the FBI. Maria de Rosario Vasquez telephoned a member of her family in Santa Ana collect, and told them such a horror story that they immediately called the police on her behalf.

Vasquez said that Sante and Ken had beaten her, forced her to work fourteen hours a day, refused to pay her, and wouldn't let her use a phone, write a letter, or speak to anyone outside their household. She couldn't leave the residence, she said, because all the doors were locked with a key from the inside.

The non-English–speaking young woman didn't know the address or city she was calling from, so the relative had the police trace the call. She had no fear that her kin would be deported. The young woman may have been Sante's first servant not brought in from Mexico as an illegal alien. Rather, police revealed, she had walked into the job voluntarily, hired from San Diego's Katrina Employment Agency on June 1. Her relatives hadn't heard from her in two months, and had filed a missing persons report before hearing from her through the collect telephone call.

Sante suspected the cops were about to arrest her. She didn't know how much they had or how severe the charges were going to be. So, she posed as a paralegal, and called a federal prosecutor, Susan King, who was helping to put the case together.

"I was trying to get off the phone and call the FBI. She was trying to get information from me," King later told *Newsday*. "She was gutsy. A real scary lady."

On Saturday morning, August 3, 1985, FBI agents swooped down on the Kimeses' condo in La Jolla and charged both Ken and Sante with "conspiracy to violate peonage and slavery laws," saying they were keeping their servants against their will, an accusation that had been made only fifteen times in the U.S. since 1977. The last time an involuntary servitude charge had occurred in California was in 1982, when the FBI had found twenty-six Indonesians who told the Feds that they had been sold as indentured servants to Beverly Hills homeowners for $3000 each.

Both Ken and Sante were soon in jail again, this time held without bond at the San Diego Metropolitan Correctional Center. Ken and Sante were advised to get separate counsel. They were each facing maximum terms of ten years in prison and $10,000 fines on sixteen separate charges.

Sante's criminal attorney, Bart Sheela III, denied the allegations. He said he hadn't read the charges, but he was absolutely sure his clients were innocent.

"I'm kind of in limbo here. But I know the Kimeses were very upset. They are amazed that anyone would do this to them."

Ken's lawyer, Frank Clemens, seemed a bit befuddled for the moment. He said he had never handled a slavery case before and only knew "the barest minimum about the case."

Since a charge of keeping slaves was so rare, the nation's press picked up the story, with Sante and Ken making the evening news on all three television networks. One reporter interviewed the Mecca Motel's manager, Marvin Parker, who said he had only met Ken once and that was when he was hired.

"He got his mail here at the motel. He stayed here for a couple of weeks when he first hired me. I haven't seen him since but I talked to him all the time on the phone," Parker said. Did Mr. Kimes have slaves working at the Mecca Motel, he was asked.

" Oh no, he doesn't do things like that. He's an upstanding, fine gentleman in all his business dealings. This is a mystery to me. All employees here are paid slightly above the minimum wage. There's no monkey business here!"

Ken stayed in the San Diego jail for three weeks, until being freed on $100,000 bail. The Feds weren't offering Sante bond at any amount. They had picked up the fur-coat conviction, and told reporters she would be expected to undergo a full mental evaluation. There would be no bail for her, they said.

The government also expanded its accusations. Ken and Sante now faced the federal charge of "involuntary servitude" plus "transporting illegal aliens, aiding and abetting, and conspiracy."

At first, the District of Columbia and Las Vegas were in a tug-of-war as to who would get to extradite Sante first. Charles Roistacher, Assistant U.S. Attorney in Washington, said he would "vigorously seek" Sante's (whose name he still misspelled as Shante) extradition to D.C. so she could be properly sentenced for the mink-coat theft. Bart Sheela said he was confident Sante would be remanded back to Las Vegas, because that was where the first complaint against her had originated. Piling it on, Roistacher said he was investigating slavery charges against her in Washington as well, as she had always traveled there with "Latino servants."

"We'll be looking into that to see if they were also held against their will," he said, full of purpose.

"Once we get her back to Las Vegas, we will be anxious to also go back to Washington to straighten that out, too," Sheela told a San Diego *Union Tribune* reporter. "Her only hope of getting out on the street again is to get all these things straightened out."

Enrique Romero, a prosecutor in the Los Angeles U.S.

Attorney's office, seemed amazed at the unfolding case. He said he didn't see slavery "happening too often. You're not in the old days of the antebellum South with chains and whips anymore."

With Sante behind bars, law officials didn't believe they would have much of a problem getting her to trial this time. She would prove them wrong.

After finally being extradited to Las Vegas, Sante was ordered continued held without bail by Nevada Judge Phillip Pro, because of her disappearing act in the Washington mink-theft conviction, and also because of the severity of the abuse charges the maids were filing against her. She spent much of her incarceration undergoing a battery of mental tests where Dr. William O'Gorman found her capable of "understanding the charges against her and she [is] able to assist in her defense."

By now, 1985 was nearly over and, after near six months behind bars, Sante undoubtedly felt that, if anything, she wasn't going to spend New Year's Eve in jail or in the mental ward of any hospital. So she did what she'd been doing for years—she grifted her way to freedom.

On the day after Christmas, Sante had been taken to the stucco southwestern-style Southern Nevada Memorial Hospital on West Charleston Boulevard for eight days of medical tests. She had conned her Clark County captors into believing she was ill, by issuing enough medical complaints to shame even the most hopeless hypochondriac. These included alleged: "pancreatic cancer, headaches, dizziness, abdominal distention, tumors, high blood pressure, sight loss, dry skin, dry scalp, swollen feet, vaginal itching, a broken toe, a dental 'condition,' numbness of the eyes, multiple head injuries, odiforous perspiration, uterine cancer, gallstones, rectal bleeding, vertigo, and mammary displasis."

After three days of cozying up to a female guard by the name of Joella Cristadora, she asked to visit a bathroom and, when Cristadora took her handcuffs and leg irons off, went inside, and while the guard waited outside the restroom, escaped.

At least that was Cristadora's first version, but that wasn't the way it happened, Nevada law authorities claimed later at a court hearing. They pointed out that there were no windows or vents inside the bathroom for Sante to have possibly squeezed her expanding girth through.

Ms. Cristadora quickly changed her story. Her second version was to tell police she had taken the leg irons off so Sante could use a telephone and, then, on the way to the bathroom, Sante began running. The guard claimed her captive had scampered all the way out the front door of the seven-story hospital and, said the gal cop, "as fast as she could run."

As might be expected, Sante had an even more dramatic tale which disputed she had ever escaped. The guard, she said, was trying to extort money from her and she had fled from her in a hospital gown. A vicious Doberman dog had attacked and chased her, she climbed a tree to escape the animal, then leaped from it to safety by landing on the other side of a fence and running away. Caked with blood from the dog bites, she hid in a parked motor home and took some old clothes from it before walking to safety.

The more likely story is that Sante simply bribed her way to freedom.

Joella Cristadora, who had quit her job the day after Sante escaped, was given blanket immunity from prosecution in an attempt to find out how Sante really fled confinement. Her testimony under oath produced this revealing exchange:

> After the December 30th escape, isn't it true you
> asked Mrs. Kimes for $7,000?"
> "No."
> "Isn't it true that your boyfriend, Paul Chandler,
> called Mrs. Kimes and asked for the money?"
> "I don't know, not to my knowledge."

Sante also had a second version of her escape. She told Chesley Goodyear, the chief deputy U.S. Marshall for Las Vegas, that Cristadora had released her because she had sympathy for her captive.

"Mrs. Kimes said the guard let her go because she had

read her story in the newspaper and didn't think she was guilty. Mrs. Kimes told her they were going to put her in a mental hospital and she would never get out," Goodyear told a court.

(According to her old friend Ruth Tanis, who was now living some 400 miles to the north in Reno, Sante called her just after breaking out and said, "I'm coming to see you." Tanis told the author she didn't know who was going to show up on her doorstep first, "the FBI or Sante." Much to Tanis' relief, neither made it to her northern Nevada home.)

Another witness who had been given immunity, Sheila Bishop, admitted she was the one who had helped to hide Sante after her escape. The Las Vegas bartender, who mixed drinks at the Elbow Room Bar at 1590 East Flamingo Road near the strip, testified that Sante had first telephoned her when she was on the run.

"She [Sante] was terrified. She said she had been through a lot and that they had let her out."

Bishop allowed that she had permitted Sante to stay in her apartment for a day or so, but then the escapee decided to move on. Bishop said FBI agents had contacted her a few days later, and she had agreed to help them apprehend the fugitive. When the escaped felon called and asked to meet with her, Bishop asked Sante to rendezvous at the Elbow Room for a drink. This time it was Sante who got conned. The FBI was waiting for her and grabbed the surprised escapee as she walked through the parking lot of the bar on her way for cocktails. Back in jail Sante would later claim all her clothes were taken away and, "I had to wrap myself in toilet paper like a mummy for warmth and modesty."

After the recapture, Sante was examined by a team of psychiatrists. She told Clifford D. O'Gorman that she was "a loving and warm person [and] a romantic who is very dependent on a man but likes it that way. I am a lover of classical music, I love to walk on the beach, and love children."

After these personal-ad–type homilies, she went into her great regret for giving up her son Kenian for adoption in Mexico. The Las Vegas shrinks were unimpressed, noting that she scored high in histrionics and narcissism.

"[Sante] has a potentially superior intelligence," wrote Verdun Trione, PhD, "but its function is disorderly, suggesting deterioration psychologically. Clinically, this is a person who snaps from time to time."

In a town where murders, million-dollar slot-machine winners, and Wayne Newton regularly compete for front-page space in its two racy papers, the trial of Sante Kimes more than held readers of the *Las Vegas Sun* and *Review-Journal* enthralled. Home slavery was a novel-enough crime that it interested even the most jaded Las Vegans, and avoiding the salacious testimony dished out by a parade of Sante's maids was like trying to look away from a traffic accident for the town's populace.

The first witness was Maria Salgado, who testified that Sante had recruited her off the streets of Mexico City when she was fourteen. Speaking through an interpreter, Salgado said that Sante had promised her parents she would be looked after. When the the girl got to California and went to work as Sante's servant, she said Sante had beaten her, spoken to her harshly, and made her work long hours.

Once, after Sante had punched her in the face, Salgado had told Sante that she possessed a strong will and promised her, "If you hit me again, I'll hit you back."

Salgado said Sante kept the telephone dismantled when she was going to be away from the house, and kept her incarcerated by locking her in. She reported eventually finding half of the phone in a bureau drawer and the other half in a closet. She put the two parts together and called her brother, who told her to flee. She liberated herself by breaking out a window and diving from it.

Another maid, a Salvadoran woman by the name of Ana Celia Soriano, said that she was originally told she would be working five days with two off, but never got any free days. When she tried to write a letter for which Sante had supplied the paper and a stamp, Sante took the missive, promising to mail it for her, but never did. She told the court that she had seen Sante taking her immigration papers from her purse and throwing them away.

Was she beaten?

"She didn't have the guts to hit me," Soriano boasted. She claimed to have dived out the window with Maria Salgado.

Still another servant, Dolores Vasquez, who was just seventeen when she testified, shed some light on how Sante had smuggled the maids into the country, having picked her up in Guadalajara, Mexico.

"We walked across the border on the beach to San Diego," she told the court in broken English. Then she gave a horrifying account of her ordeal.

"She hit me because I burned the hamburger bread. On another occasion, *la Señora* threatened me with a pistol. She called me stupid," Vasquez said.

The girl saved her most excruciating testimony for the end, telling of an incident in a hotel suite when she was traveling with the Kimes family.

"I had an allergy. My pressure go up and I fainted. *La Señora* said to go into the shower. All of a sudden she would steam up like that. I had taken off my clothes and she told me to get in the shower. I put the water on lukewarm. She changed the water to very hot. It burned. When I moved away to a corner of the bathtub, she threw hot water on me with a little pot."

The teen testified in court that Sante had told her she couldn't leave because the U.S. and Mexico "were having problems."

Maribel Cruz Ramirez, another illegal immigrant, said that Sante had burned her with an iron and locked her in a closet overnight. Dominic Gentile, Sante's most vocal defense lawyer at the trial, tried to put the best face on the pile of evidence as voiced by her victims.

"They got all the necessities of life for compensation. If they were paid money, they couldn't have done as well," he blustered.

Ken wasn't present in the courtroom. Papa Kimes had by now already cut a deal with the FBI, and had pled guilty. In exchange, he was guaranteed no jail time, as long as he paid a $70,000 fine, accepted a three-year suspended sentence, and agreed to enter a long-term treatment program for alcoholics.

For her part, Sante attempted to play the role of martyr throughout the trial. She kept a box of tissues in front of her and, when the maids got to their tales of torture, she would alternately cry or dab at her eyes, as if in sympathy with their pain. Her lawyers at least managed to tone down her appearance. She showed up for the trial wearing conservative, neutral-colored, housewife-type dresses.

But the evidence was both overwhelming and damning. Amalia Osorio, the teen who had escaped over Sante's Las Vegas wall, said "the lady hit me and slapped me in the face because I burned her pants" after promising the servant $200 a week but never paying her a penny. The prosecution followed that by producing a tutor, Melody Keltz, who corroborated Osario's claim and added to it.

"I saw Amalia's hair being pulled and saw her spanked."

"Who did you see doing this?" Keltz was asked.

"Sante Kimes."

Prosecutor Michael Stuhff brought on witness after witness, each of whom had a horror story that seemed to top the one before it. One maid, Adela Sanchez, (see Appendix D), told of being beaten with belt buckles and coat hangers. Another young girl spoke of having to strip naked for an inspection, being thrown over an ironing board, and then being deliberately burnt with a hot steam iron by Sante. She showed the still-fresh scar to the jury.

Sante's defense attorneys produced a barrage of character witnesses who all swore that Mrs. Kenneth Kimes was a kind and loving woman who kept her doors locked from the inside because she was frightened of her husband's relatives.

One friend, Sandra Spears, claimed Sante's office had been broken into and a message had been scrawled across its walls.

"A threat—I forget the words—but a threat was written in red on the walls. It looked like blood. And there was a picture of a person hanging with a noose around his neck."

Mrs. Kimes' pal also told the same snake anecdote that

Sante had been telling on Ken's daughter, Linda, with relish for years.

"She was as white as a ghost, frightened out of her wits. Her eyes were like saucers. Someone had put live rattlesnakes in her car!"

Spears also added that her good friend, Mrs. Kimes, was pregnant during the rattlesnake incident.

"The maids never made any derogatory comments ever that I heard about Mrs. Kimes," said another defender, Sante's travel agent, Luis Rumis. "The maids had the chance to say they were unhappy, but they never did."

The most vocal champion for Sante was Grant Christopherson, who, a dozen years later, would, with his wife, tell *Dateline NBC* that Sante had stolen his stationery and parked stolen cars in his driveway. In this trial, however, he buttressed the death-by-rattlesnakes story, adding that when Sante "discovered rattlesnakes in the car, she couldn't get the door open and had to break the window to get out."

After repeating the blood-on-the-walls-in-the-office tale as well, Christopherson told the jury that Sante lived in fear that her relatives wanted to either abduct or harm Kenny and, he testified, this was the reason for her many aliases.

"They moved from hotel to hotel to assure themselves privacy. Sometimes they registered under different names to make sure their enemies, the creeps, were not aware of her or where she was," Christopherson testified.

Under cross-examination, Christopherson admitted he had no personal knowledge of any of the incidents and had never met any of the "creeps" or the relatives he accused. His wife also testified, implying that Ken's family wanted his money.

"Her husband was an extremely wealthy man," Pat Christopherson said, "and apparently money was the name of the game."

Both said that the maids appeared free to leave but, as Mr. Christopherson said, "because of her limited English, they probably didn't go out much."

The prosecutor rebutted the Christophersons' testimony with a Las Vegas restaurant owner, Chris Karamanos, who said they *had* tried to get out—a lot. He spoke emotionally, saying that an escaped maid had come to his door and pleaded with him in Spanish. Seeing that she was frightened, he tried to help her. When he went to the Kimes house to get her things, Sante greeted him at the door with a stream of obscenities, claiming the maid had a contract with her and, thus, couldn't leave. Karamanos said Sante quieted down and apologized after he threatened to call the police. The cafe operator testified he drove the girl to the Las Vegas airport and that he paid for a ticket back to San Diego for the servant.

With the trial winding down, Sante's defense team's best chance was for a mistrial. When a juror told the judge he had overheard the other jurors discussing Ken Kimes, her chief lawyer, Dominic Gentile, almost managed to get the case thrown out.

Judge Howard McKibben had forbidden the jury to discuss Sante's husband, and so he polled the fourteen-person box. Ten of them admitted hearing a discussion of Ken but none admitted to being the one who had brought him up. All of them said it would not prejudice their feelings towards the defendant.

"Almost everyone heard the comment," protested Sante's lawyer to a Las Vegas reporter, "but no one admitted he said it."

The judge admonished the jury from discussing the case and allowed the summations to begin.

"Sante Kimes is a greedy, cunning and cruel woman who thought she was above the law," one of her prosecutors, Karla Dobinski, began in a strong voice. "She lied to these maids to get them to go with her. She coerced them to stay with her by overcoming their will."

Dobinski said Sante had lured them with promises of a decent salary, days off, and continued contact with relatives, but had kept none of her vows. Instead, she said, Sante had forced the maids to work continuously, would not let them communicate with their loved ones, and created such fear in them they were afraid to leave. The prosecutor went into a litany of abuses in which she said Sante had either slapped, beaten, or threatened the young girls in order to keep them silent and compliant.

Then Dobinski read typewritten orders that Sante had given to each servant that began, ominously, "You better be happy here. We are your family and you will be here permanently."

Sante also made the girls call her Mama, the prosecutor said.

As Dobinski continued, Sante began sobbing, and as the prosecutor recounted the maid's tale of her being burnt with a hot iron, Sante interrupted her argument by crying out.

"These are lies! It is all lies!" she shouted.

Judge McKibben declared a recess so that Sante could calm herself down. Karla Dobinski wasn't rattled by Sante's outburst. She continued hammering home her closing points as soon as the court reconvened.

"Sante Kimes was smart enough not to let on to family friends of the dark side of her household. The beatings were behind closed doors. The defense showed you snapshots of apparently happy girls, but the cameras weren't rolling during the beatings."

Dobinski said many of the young girls had been brought into the country illegally by Kenny's tutors.

"She [Sante] told the tutors to select young, naive, and unsophisticated girls who spoke only Spanish and had no papers to be in the states legally. She recruited subservient girls because she could have more power over them."

Dominic Gentile, speaking on behalf of Sante, surprisingly didn't seem to care much for his client, and attempted to base his argument on legalities.

"I'm not asking you to hug Sante Kimes and bring her into your living room," he began. "Even if you think Sante Kimes is a bitch, you still have to follow the law."

With that lefthanded opening, Gentile said that not enough evidence had been presented to convict her because the maids voluntarily came to work for her in her houses and they generally did not retaliate after they left the Kimes household.

"Economic necessity may cause a person to accept a job she may not want to perform," Gentile argued. "While this may seem like that person is being kept there under coercion, it is not involuntary servitude.

"There's a lot of difference between not being happy with your work and involuntary servitude. The maids and the tutors, for that matter, worked for food, shelter, and travel. The tutors weren't paid, and, yet, Sante Kimes was able to get these college-educated teachers to go to work for her under these terms.

"Mrs. Kimes was their employer. She doesn't owe them an explanation of her conduct. If they don't like it, they can hit the door."

Sante was strict and secretive with her servants, Gentile's theory went, because her husband's relatives were trying to harm her and her young son.

"To preserve the security of her family and her son, Mrs. Kimes had to do things that were extraordinary," her lawyer told the court.

Then, Gentile began waving a pair of leg shackles and handcuffs around, saying this was the kind of force that constituted a conviction of enslaving people.

"Isn't this what we mean by involuntary servitude?" Gentile shouted, holding up the metal restraints. "Chains, retaliation, incarceration—these are the badges of slavery. There was none of that in this case!"

Sante's lawyer accused the maids of being motivated by greed. He hinted that the real reason some of the maids had testified against her was because they had a multimillion dollar lawsuit in the works against Sante and her husband. He even excused Sante's disappearance from the locked hospital ward on the basis that her guard had permitted her to leave.

"This is a wages case, perhaps. Maybe it's a battering case. Yes, Mrs. Kimes did lose her temper a few times. If the maids are entitled to money, let them go to civil court. But this not a slavery case."

Karla Dobinski's partner, assistant U.S. Attorney Stephen Clark, rebutted Gentile's argument forcefully.

"This defendant does not deserve your sympathy. She's a skilled actress and a skilled liar. She can and will do anything to keep from taking responsibility for her actions.

"The fact that these girls had to escape, sometimes in the middle of the night, is the best evidence they were being held against their will. The maids ran away in terror and sometimes, even though they were illegal aliens, they went straight to federal authorities. It strains credibility to think of these poor illegal aliens as willing to work away from home, out of touch with relatives, without any pay or days off, merely for the opportunity to travel."

Clark said any argument about real or imagined enemies trying to harm her family wasn't even relevant. Sante's eleven-day slavery trial was over.

Chapter Twelve

A Body (or Two) Disappears

On the last day of February 1986, the U.S. District Court in Las Vegas found Sante Kimes guilty of fourteen of the sixteen counts that charged her with keeping slaves, transporting illegal aliens into the United States, escaping from prison, and conspiracy. The two charges that got dismissed were because a couple of the maids were in her employ fewer than five days. Sante, wearing a severe pearl-gray (some wags said prison-gray) dress and flanked by her two lawyers, Dominic Gentile and Michael Stuhff, was emotionless. Her tormentors were not. The two prosecutors, Karla Dobinski and Stephen Clark, broke out in celebratory smiles as the verdict was read. Neither Ken nor little Kenny was present.

The *Las Vegas Sun* headlined the decision—KIMES GUILTY IN SLAVE CASE—across the top of the entire front page in its March 1 edition. The size of the type was large enough for a declaration of war.

In mid-April, both Ken and Sante were sentenced. By now, Sante had parted ways with Gentile and Stuhff, and a new attorney was representing her, Oscar Goodman. He pleaded with Judge McKibben for leniency, noting she was "a troubled woman" who should be placed in a special facility for psychiatric treatment rather than prison.

Karla Dobinski was not in the mood for leniency that day. She reminded the justice that Sante had "committed very serious crimes of violence and physical abuse for a longstanding period of time."

Ken Kimes also had a new lawyer, famed Los Angeles attorney Howard Weitzman, who had already made his reputation by defending John Delorean, and would go on to represent both Michael Jackson and O. J. Simpson (he parted ways with his client three days after the murder of the sportscaster's wife), before becoming an executive at Universal Pictures. It was Weitzman who helped broker Ken's guilty plea, which let him off with a suspended sentence, a fine, and the alcohol-treatment plan. For getting Papa Kimes off, sources told the author, he was very handsomely paid.

"Your crime is one of omission, not commission," Judge McKibbben lectured him. "I can't condone your activities. I think the message sent out by this court is that it will not tolerate this kind of conduct."

McKibben, who then sentenced Sante, said that she had "some fairly deep-seated psychological problems." He noted the reports from two of the psychiatrists indicated Sante needed therapy, and reported she "suffered from family emotional disturbances." But, he said, "that does not excuse you from your reprehensible acts.

"You engaged in the longstanding activity of bring illegal aliens to this country. You have little concern for the laws of the United States and continued to violate the law."

He gave Sante five years, the maximum term. She was sent first to the federal correctional facility in Lexington, Kentucky, and, later, a women's minimum security federal correctional center in Alameda County, California, near San Francisco.

Friends of Kenny all agree that he seemed to thrive with his mother away at "Club Fed," as Sante referred to her new situation. His father may have indulged his son, but at least there was no longer any rancor or tension omnipresent in the Kimes household. Kenny was sent to school for the first time, entering Saint Viator's Catholic elementary school as a sixth-grader. Big Ken spoiled him by installing a swimming pool, and taking his son and the neighborhood kids to McDonald's, paying for everything. Once, he chauffeured a group of Kenny's pals to Beverly Hills and rented hotel suites for them, where the boys were allowed luxuries like breakfast in bed and shopping tours of Rodeo Drive. To help pay his trial costs, he raised some short-term cash by selling the Mecca Motel for $3.4 million six months after the trial.

Sante wasn't forgotten completely. They wouldn't have dared. The two Kens visited her in prison. Sante demanded it and, for all her transgressions, she was still able to cast a magic spell over her husband. But Kenny made a weak try at cutting back his dependence on his mother.

"He was ashamed of her," his best pal Vittorio Raho would tell the *New York Times*. "He didn't even want to talk to her on the phone."

"He told me he hated his mom," another boyhood buddy recalled. "He said she was crazy."

Sante was certainly good for some tall tales of life in the slammer. Some of her dramatic anecdotes were right out of nineteenth-century-prison horror fiction.

"I have been attacked and beaten," she wrote from jail. "I have crouched in freezing cells with rats. I have had my hair ripped and cut off while trying to help a pregnant inmate who was being mercilessly beaten."

She also claimed she had been pushed down a flight of stairs ten days after arriving in the federal prison system. That had caused a concussion, she said.

Sante would also say she had found a new love while working in the prison law library. She began to bemoan the fact she had never become a lawyer.

"A whole new world has opened," she wrote from the inside. "I can only say I wish I had been an attorney and defended the laws of my country instead of being ignorant of them and breaking them. I know I'm not a criminal type person, and hope I am never considered to be like some of the people I'm in contact with here."

Despite her newfound love of the law, Sante was anything but a model prisoner. Records show she was disciplined for breaking rules nine times, possessed contraband on two occasions, disobeyed orders, and spent fifteen days in solitary confinement.

*   *   *

A year after Sante went off to jail, Kenny graduated from elementary school and entered a combination parochial middle school and high school in Las Vegas called Bishop Gorman. He was becoming a normal boy. Ken's son started to become interested in both girls and computers. Sante began to plead for an early release based on not being able to be with her "three" sons, even though one had been given up for adoption and the other was an adult.

"I am missing the cutest phases of Kenian's toddler years and the difficult and sensitive stages of Kenny's entering puberty, missing the darling times when youngsters make all sorts of darling discoveries, watching their little faces light up with joy of learning new things . . . Kenny is ridiculed in school and is the brunt of many cruel jokes. And I am not there to ease the blow or dry his tears . . ."

Sante's own crocodile tears aside, she also came on as someone determined not to let her current situation get her down. She compared her suffering to being in a concentration camp in one maudlin letter.

"Miraculously, I am not destroyed. I am determined to come through this Holocaust a stronger and much wiser person," she wrote.

Sante also spent her years in prison still battling her maids from her cell. Adela Sanchez and several other former servants had launched a lawsuit against both Mr. and Mrs. Kimes. They asked for a total of $35 million, which could have bankrupted Ken had they won. Sante's contention was that her homeowner's insurance should take care of it and pay off their claims. From prison, Sante engaged more than fifty lawyers to sue her household insurer, though many failed to get paid.

"You can be insured if a person trips and falls down on your front porch," an attorney who opposed Sante, Jeff Portnoy, would say. "We don't insure people for keeping slaves."

Portnoy was wrong. The insurance companies soon capitulated and paid off the maids for an undisclosed amount, amazing the attorney.

"This is someone who is capable of doing virtually anything to get what she wants," Portnoy concluded.

Sante always maintained her innocence in the involuntary servitude matter. In one almost delusional diatribe from her correctional center, she tearfully told lawyers suing on behalf of her former household help: "It's intolerable being away from your children. Especially when you're wrongly convicted and you've done nothing wrong like I have in my case. I've suffered brain concussions and injuries. I have been wrongly incarcerated for three years. I never yelled loudly [at the maids] and I'm certain I never physically touched any of them."

While Sante was in prison, Ken, now more than seventy years of age, began to put his affairs in order. Although he was afraid *not* to allow Sante back into his life, he began taking steps to see that much of his still formidable fortune would go to his children—particularly those from his first marriage—and not Sante. He undoubtedly knew that Sante, nearly two decades younger, would try to control those assets after his demise. To thwart her, he began squirreling away millions of dollars in secret offshore banking accounts in the Commonwealth of the Bahamas and other Caribbean islands that had laws assuring privacy.

After entering a thirty-eight-page motion for early release in late 1988 in which she promised, "I will never break another law as long as I live . . . I hate myself for my stupidity and ignorance," a self-described "contrite" Sante got out of prison in early 1989. Kenny Kimes' "golden years" were over.

Sometimes life imitates art and sometimes it's the other way around. In the final scene of *The Grifters*—the 1990 film about a mother and son who are both con artists—there is a fight in which the mother rushes toward her son, who is holding a glass. It shatters between them and a jagged edge accidentally slashes his jugular vein during their brutal battle. The son quickly bleeds to death and, after a few tears, the mother turns away from his body, to continue her grifting profession.

When Sante arrived home from prison in 1989, a similar scene occurred between her and Kenny. She had asserted herself over Ken "Papa" Kimes and their son once again, insisting they move to another part of Las Vegas, and yanking Kenny out of his Catholic high school. Then, she attempted to forbid him from associating with the friends he had made while she was away.

Kenny, nearly fifteen, erupted in anger. He attacked his mother physically in an outpouring of the perpetual love-hate relationship that had always been a bond between them. Sante was unable to simply cower or run away, but fought back, using her nails to scratch and claw Kenny. When the violent test of wills was over, there were tears amid a blotting up of the blood that had been shed, but at least neither had killed the other. It was just after that traumatic moment, Kenny would later tell friends, he realized that despite what his mother was drawing him into, he could never leave her. Somehow, they would always be together.

"It's like, she's my mother, man," he would later tell his boyhood friend Vittorio Raho, when Raho asked him why he continued to stay by her side.

He dropped out of school, and went back to life with the tutors, an increasingly feeble father, and an even more domineering Sante. Sante rewarded his good behavior by taking everyone on a grand tour of Europe and Asia. His mother, rootless for much of her life, was still able to work her will on her aged husband, and soon on her impressionable son. She attempted to pay for the long and expensive vacation from the insurance proceeds of their house in Hawaii, which she had instructed a friend and lawyer, Elmer A. Holmgren, to burn to the ground.

Sante had hired Chicago native Elmer Holmgren in Las Vegas, a year after she was released from prison. Holmgren had been the claims supervisor for the insurance company that had paid off on their 1978 Hawaiian house fire. She put the lawyer on retainer. He soon found out that working for Sante involved more than shuffling legal papers. Part of his job was to take the fall for Sante. If the law got too close, it was Holmgren's job to plead incompetence, saying he had lost critical evidence, or Sante would have him go into hiding and then go to court and say her lawyer had "run off with the evidence."

On Labor Day weekend of 1990, Papa Kimes could be seen driving off with some of the family's furniture and personal possessions, loaded into a rented truck. A few days later, Holmgren torched the house. Holmgren had a drinking problem and, a few weeks following the fire, after he had downed one too many vodkas, admitted to a drinking buddy that he was the one who set the Kimeses' house on fire. He did it, he said, so Sante could get the insurance money. His buddy ratted on him to the police, who then wired him and got Holmgren's arson confession on tape. The law could now make the lawyer toil for them.

Holmgren was forced to became a double agent, working for both the Kimes and the U.S. Bureau of Alcohol, Firearms, and Tobacco. But Holmgren couldn't keep his mouth shut. He began telling friends that he would be going into the Fed's witness-protection program when his days as a mole were over. He may have talked too much.

In January 1991, Sante and her husband asked the fifty-nine-year-old alcoholic to join them on a working vacation to Costa Rica, telling Holmgren they wanted him along because they might be looking at some land.

The attorney was worried. He called his son, Kenneth.

"He sounded distressed," his son recalled. "He said if I didn't hear from him in three days to call the Honolulu office of the ATF. That was the last thing I ever heard from him."

Holmgren never returned from Costa Rica with Sante and big Ken. And, when Holmgren's son called the ATF, the embarrassed agents refused to discuss the subject with him.

The burning down of the Hawaiian oceanfront mansion for quick cash turned out to be an exercise in futility. Their insurance companies were on to Sante now. The insurer of the house, The Chubb Corporation, refused to pay off on both the fire and the Kimeses' additonal claim that the house had been burglarized, and the furniture stolen, just before the blaze began. The suspicious 1978 fire and the discovery of the Kimeses' arrest and conviction records by the company's investigators were more than enough for Chubb to deny them any payment. A crazed, angry Sante sued the insurance firm and then flew to Chubb's New Jersey headquarters in an attempt to get executives to give her the money.

She began by casing their Warren, New Jersey, corporate headquarters, posing as a location scout for ABC's popular soap opera *All My Children*. As an *AMC* agent, Sante used the alias Sandra Chambers, a ruse that surely must have made her adoptive mother revolve once or twice in her grave.

After studying Chubb's home office and learning the home address of Chubb's chief executive officer, Dean O'Hare, Sante showed up at his Far Hills, New Jersey, home brandishing a bouquet of white lilies—a symbol of death. The frightened O'Hare family hired bodyguards.

Sante next followed O'Hare to a convention in San Francisco, where she began telephoning him in his hotel room repeatedly, starting before daybreak. She also made a series of calls to O'Hare's wife. Both of the O'Hares were implored to pay Sante off, using the "Hawaiian Mafia/Hawaiian Crime Syndicate" conspiracy tale as the real reason for her house burning down. Sante may have even tried to use some of her "black magic" spells. The O'Hare security guards would report "a prowler" on the premises of the O'Hare house at three in the morning in 1991. The next morning, they found a large black crow next to Mrs. O'Hare's sedan.

Sante finally got face time with O'Hare after conning her way into his offices and telling the building's receptionist that she had an appointment with Chubb's public-relations department. O'Hare, who later sued Sante for harassment, would testify that Sante had at least obliquely threatened the life of his family.

"Mrs. Kimes moved close to me, stared in my eyes, and told me of a friend's seventeen-year-old son, whose body was dismembered and sent to his father in pieces. She further told me of her friend's twelve-year-old son, who disappeared and was never seen again . . . She said this is the treatment of people who upset the Hawaiian Crime Syndicate," O'Hare told an attorney in a sworn deposition.

O'Hare's sons were seventeen and twelve. The Chubb CEO eventually got an injunction that prevented Sante from

harassing him further. Sante gave up soon after that and
dropped her suit for payment.

After their world tour, Sante and Ken could no longer
live in Las Vegas. The Kimes family had been shunned
before. But Sante (and Ken's) conviction—with the resulting notoriety in the press—for keeping slaves in her household had marked her as a scarlet woman even in the
generally tolerant gambling capital. With her ability to scam
insurance companies constricted because of her exposed police record and long history of dubious claims, Sante's income stream from that corner had dried up. Ken no longer
had the ability to spend as freely as he had in the past. He
was, in his words, "cash poor." The claim was true, as he
had now hidden a large portion of his liquid assets in offshore bank accounts. However, Sante also knew of the other
half of his fortune—large tracts of raw California land in
great locations, some of which he had owned for more than
three decades. One prime piece, which Sante felt was ripe
for building on, was the old Wheat Ranch Development in
Santa Barbara County, near the town of Santa Maria. Ken
had bought it when he was married to Charloette and had
been awarded the property as part of the divorce spoils.

Sante, Ken, and Kenny moved to Montecito, a village of
10,000 just south of the city of Santa Barbara. The municipality is one of California's most picturesque small towns,
some 100 miles up the Pacific Coast Highway from Los
Angeles. Sante began telling people around town that she
was an alumna of the University of California at Santa Barbara and had moved there in order to groom her son to
follow in her footsteps at UCSB. Mrs. Kimes also talked
about wanting to develop some nearby real estate she
owned.

Sante already had a patsy in the town. She had met Santa
Barbara resident and retired schoolteacher John Boettner and
his wife in a Las Vegas casino. Sante at first asked Boettner
if she would tutor Kenny so he could pass an exam to get
into UCSB, since he was missing a formal high-school diploma. She next asked Boettner if she could use his Rock
Creek Road address to receive mail while they awaited set-

tlement on a new house they were buying. After Boettner agreed to the request, Sante had his address printed on her checks, and gave the former teacher's address and name as the resident agent for Kimes Construction, Inc., and on other legal documents, all without Boettner's knowledge.

A nervous Boettner, who talked to the author in the fall of 1998, denied he had been Kenny's tutor, instead saying he had "just found them a tutor." Boettner said he was so upset by his name being put on real-estate documents without his knowledge that he had hired a local lawyer to straighten out the legal nightmare for him.

Sante began getting bids to survey the Wheat Ranch property and subdivide the land into 170 lots for a housing development. She would have the title for the property transferred from Kenneth Kimes to her name in 1993. Members of the Kimes family have challenged this transfer on the grounds that the signature of Ken Kimes is a possible forgery. After getting the title in her name, Sante transferred the title to a Nevada Corporation "owned" by her friend, David Kazdin, and then back to her again to muddy the paper trail. (Kazdin's body would be found in a Los Angeles Dumpster in March 1998 by a homeless man searching for recyclable aluminum cans to be turned in to a salvage dump and exchanged for cash.)

Kenny entered the University of California at Santa Barbara with a new four-wheel-drive Jeep and no declared major. He began living at Santa Cruz Residence Hall. The author, who talked with those who knew him at UCSB about his courses, got vague answers, generally "poly-sci" or "computers." According to school records, he took a light class load, but appeared to be doing decently, according to those who thought of Kenny as their friend during his college years.

During the noon hour, on March 28, 1994, Kenneth Keith Kimes waited for Sante with his stepson Kent Walker outside a Santa Barbara bank in a new Lincoln they had just purchased. Inside the financial institution, his companion of two decades was making a withdrawal. When she came back to the car, he was dead. Still, Sante had Kent—who would claim to New York newspapers in 1998 that he was "estranged" from her—call an ambulance to take Papa Kimes to Goleta Valley Hospital in a vain attempt to revive him. The emergency room's doctors and all of Sante's "black magic" couldn't bring him back. His soulmate said her final goodbyes while slipping the big diamond ring that was a symbol of his wealth off his finger. The next day, she showed up in the Santa Barbara coroner's office, threatening to sue the county because the ambulance didn't get her husband to the hospital fast enough.

Papa Kimes was seventy-seven when he died. The Santa Barbara coroner called it a "massive hemorrhage," caused by a "ruptured abdominal aortic aneurysm." On the death certificate (*see* Exhibit B), Sante embellished her husband's background, saying he had four years of college when, in fact, he had none. She also told the coroner's office the first name of Ken's father was Keith instead of Charles, and spelled his mother's name Naomi instead of Neoma, and also reported her maiden name was Wardshaw, all inaccuracies. The address Sante gave as their main residence was a commercial mail drop in Las Vegas. Most curious of all was the Social Security number Sante gave as her husband's. It was not only wrong, but it was the number of *another* Kenneth Kimes—a very much alive resident of Los Angeles.

Sante did not tell Ken's children or his former wife or any of his friends that her partner was gone. As far as the public was concerned, Papa Kimes was still alive. When relatives and business friends would call to inquire, she would tell them he was "away in the Bahamas" or "building a hotel in Japan." She tried to hide his will. There was nothing in it for her, and Sante felt that she and Kenny deserved not just something but everything. Ken had written the will before he met his companion of more than twenty-two years, the woman he had often referred to as his wife. It had never been updated. On top of all that, much of the the money was squirreled away in secret Caribbean bank accounts.

She had to tell Kenny. Her son was away on his first

college spring break. When he came back, Sante was there at the airport to meet him.

"Where's Papa?" Kenny asked, looking around.

"He's right here," Sante told her son, and in a macabre move worthy of a Stephen King novel showed him the urn with his father's ashes inside. Kenny later told his friends he was as much devastated by the way he learned of his father's demise as the death itself. Then Sante made Kenny jump right back on a plane to Hawaii. There they took the cinders that had once been Kenneth Keith Kimes and scattered them on the waves that lapped the shoreline in front of their torched home.

By the time they got back to Santa Barbara his mother was prepared to do anything she had to do in order to keep control of Ken's $12 million fortune.

Anything.

Chapter Thirteen

The Son (also) Rises

"Kenny said when his father died he pretty much knew he was going to be in trouble," another of Kenny's former friends, twenty-two-year-old Nader Helmi, once told *Time*. "His mother was lying to Kenny's father about things. It was pretty obvious she was doing things to people. Kenny knew and his dad didn't."

When Vittorio Raho explained to Helmi that Sante and Kenny had become very, very close, Helmi said, "That's weird."

Raho shrugged.

"Yeah, it's weird, but maybe it's a good thing."

Shortly after the death of Papa Kimes, Sante tried to boost Kenny's self-esteem by treating him to a nose job. Kenny had inherited his dad's hooked Roman nose and, with Big Ken's ashes at the bottom of the Pacific, there was no longer anyone around for Sante to offend by altering her boy's bumpy beak. Kenny's mom needed to go into the shop for an overhaul herself. Hard living and three years of hard time had worked her over so badly she was becoming a walking wattle.

While staying at her Cable Beach home near Nassau in the Bahama Islands, Sante had seen some TV commercials by a San Diego plastic surgeon. The doctor, Joseph P. Graves, M.D., was a man that a woman like Sante could identify with—he even had an alias, Joseph P. Limoli. Graves was advertising on television, saying he was a California Board-Certified surgeon, and a former instructor at Stanford University Medical School. In fact, he was neither. In delicious irony, Sante and Kenny were about to be conned by a con. Doctor Graves would later be forced to surrender his medical license on July 7, 1998, by the Medical Board of California, two days after Sante and Kenny's New York arrest.

Among the several charges alleged against Graves by the state of California were unprofessional conduct and false advertising. One of his clients, "Brenda T," nearly died from an excessive liposuction surgery after Graves had told the five-foot-four 230-pound woman she was to be "his little protege." He then proceeded to suck out 11,000 cc of fat, an amount so vastly exceeding guidelines that she vomited continuously and had trouble breathing. Another disastrous operation was on "Kristin L," in which both breast implants installed by Graves ruptured, with the woman's breasts leaking blood and left with excessive scarring.

The Medical Board of California eventually determined that Graves was a "manic depressive" suffering from "bipolar effective disorder" and "paranoia, irrationality, and self-destructive behaviour." If ever Sante and Kenny had cause to sue for a mangled operation this would have been their time. And, according to reports, what an incompetent piece of surgery it indeed turned out to be.

Sante, who found it necessary to portray herself to Graves as a "mature model" (perhaps she was angling for a discount), contracted for a facelift, with the loose skin around her neck to be removed and then tightened, adding a liposuction procedure for good measure. Kenny just asked for his nose to be sculpted, and the bump removed. Both operations were a mess. Kenny's nose looked worse after the procedure than before it. And, Sante learned from a nurse that while under the anaesthesia, she had fallen off the operating table, injuring her face, and nearly had her eye put out by a tool box sitting on the floor. Graves panicked and went into a depressive state. He wouldn't take Sante to a hospital, instead dumping her and Kenny back at their La Jolla hotel.

Both mother and son sued for malpractice and certainly

had a good case, but Graves wouldn't settle out of court. When the doctor's lawyer, Joseph Lange, scheduled them for a routine deposition, neither showed. Sante's long history of lawsuits, suspected arson, and a criminal history had stripped her of any credibility. The lawsuit, perhaps the only valid one of her life, was dismissed.

The following summer, after a second year at UCSB, Sante decided that Kenny should follow his father into the construction business. Big Ken had known Michael Towbes, who headed a large commercial and residential building firm in Santa Barbara under the name The Towbes Group. Sante was promising the construction company preferential treatment for the Santa Maria project, so Sante went to Towbes and used her influence to get Kenny a summer job. She was sent to the company's human-resources department.

"I thought it was Tammy Faye Bakker walking in the door," a supervisor in the firm's human-resources offices told the author, remembering Sante's entrance in what she called "a flowing chiffon gown. All that makeup and blue eye shadow and the intense, reeking perfume. I had to air out my office when she left!"

The source said that Sante wanted to know what Kenny would be paid for the summer job. When his mother was told $6.50 an hour, she became upset.

"My son is worth twenty dollars an hour," she fumed. When she was told again that the amount wasn't possible for a student intern being hired essentially to run errands and file or refile blueprints, Kenny's mom worked out a unique solution.

"You pay him twenty and bill me the difference," Sante ordered, adding she'd make up the difference in the taxes as well. The human-resource employee, with the approval of management, did so, according to the source, with Kenny never finding out.

Said the Towbes Group supervisor, "Kenny didn't seem all that bright. He liked to talk about the stock market a lot but he knew nothing about computers."

Kenny quickly proved to be inept at simple tasks, and also seemed to have his wires crossed when it came to polite conversation. When a notorious soft-core porno film opened in Santa Barbara he remarked to a young woman in the office that the film "looked like a great date movie."

As Kara Craver-Jones had noted, he still lacked "social skills."

The Towbes Group let him go before the end of summer, partly because there was little work for him to do, but mostly because he couldn't always accomplish even the most menial of assignments. When she heard about the firing, Sante became incensed. She demanded to meet with the someone from human resources at a nearby bar to find out what had gone wrong. The employee refused to meet with her, so Sante instead wrote a long, florid letter denouncing the firm, writing the document as if the deceased Ken "Papa" Kimes was still alive. The last paragraph read.

Papa and I have tried to install certain rules of life within Kenny. They are truthfulness, faithfulness, enthusiasm, perseverance, energy, humility, and excellence at everything we do, with a zest for living.

Kenny eventually got thrown out of the residence hall he was living in at UCSB for fighting with another student. His opponent was hurt badly enough to be treated at a local hospital. After the dust-up, he was barred from entering any student housing on campus, but still attempted to continue his college experience. For a short time after the fight, he stayed with Alan and Trish Kadje. Trish's husband was a Santa Barbara cop. Both grew to love the hulking man-child, advising him to break off his close ties with his mother. Displaying a cop's instinct, the Kadjes thought his mom was a hardened criminal and eventually would "drag him down with her."

Trish Kadje got upset with Kenny continued kowtowing to Sante. "Stand up to your mother," she counseled.

At the beginning of the 1994-95 school year, Kenny tried again. This time, he rented a large apartment with five other students on Trigo Road in Goleta, a bedroom community just north of Santa Barbara. Kenny's share of the $1920 monthly rent was $320.

In spite of living a few miles away from her son, Sante remained very much in Kenny's life. Kenny seemed to take turns alternately being proud of his mom, trotting her out as a delightful eccentric, or being greatly ashamed of her. Once, when a classmate asked him about Sante's origins, he hung his head and seemed on the edge of tears.

"My mother? Man, you don't want to know about my mother," Kenny said softly.

Yet it was Sante and Kenny who jointly hosted a "back-to-school" celebration in September 1995, perhaps one of the few times in college history that a mother and son presided over a keg party together. In an affidavit filed by Bill Pallo describing the festivities, Sante appears to be ordering the youths around, telling them that "only one person is allowed in the bathroom," after one young lady is accused of "going back and forth into the bathroom with three different guys." At the same party Pallo describes a young woman "with her skirt so short that you could see her panties as she walked." What kind of college bacchanal Sante and Ken was hosting is not made clear.

The affidavit is part of a voluminous court document that describes Kenny's next hint of an emerging violent personality. The complainant, UCSB law student Carrie Louise Grammer, would file this letter with Judge Thomas R. Adams in an attempt to get a restraining order against Kenny Kimes on October 25, 1995.

> *The person I am filing this restraining order against*
> *is Ken Kimes. I have known him for over a year. We both*
> *lived in Santa Cruz Residence Hall the last school year,*
> *and at one time I had considered him to be a friend. My*
> *boyfriend, Pat Lieneweg, has known Ken for over two*
> *years, and is one of Ken's housemates this school year.*
> *Pat also had considered Ken to be a friend.*
>
> *At one time I had thought Ken to be a decent person.*
> *He is very charismatic, but over the past few months, I*
> *have realized that his charming behavior is an inten-*
> *tional cover to hide his true abusive personality. As of*

this past weekend (10/13–10/15) I am afraid of Ken.

I need to explain the events which led to the actual incident that made me fear Ken.

A few weeks ago, Ken brought his cat to my apartment to be watched for a few hours. The cat soiled my roommate's bed, which cost her seventy dollars to replace the soiled bedding, to which Ken agreed to reimburse the entire amount. When my roommate, [Lauren Schmalbach] and I arrived at Ken's apartment. to collect the money, Evan Dienstag, one of the housemates, answered the door and gave me thirty-five dollars, saying Ken had instructed him to give the money to us. Lauren and I told Evan that we wanted to speak to Ken, so Evan let us in. Ken's door was shut. But when Ken heard me ask Evan if he [Ken] had locked himself in his room, Ken flung his door open. I walked in to see Ken sitting at his desk counting money. I could see that he had well over $100 in large bills. Ken was putting on a show for me. Ken is financially very well off and he was flaunting the money in an attempt to anger me.

I asked why he would not pay Lauren. He said he was not going to pay and told me that if our friendship was worth only thirty-five dollars then I can "fuck off." I said to Ken that he was being an "asshole." Ken immediately jumped out of his chair. He came at me in a threatening manner with an infuriated expression on his face. His eyes were squinted, his jaw stuck out, his lips were pinched, and his face was red. Ken is very large, he lifts weights everyday. Ken is 6'2" and weighs about 200 pounds. I am five-foot tall and weigh 115 pounds. I immediately became very frightened. Ken stood over me and with his finger pointed at my face, he proceeded to angrily curse at me. From this point on, everything Ken said contained excessive profanity. Ken's eyes looked crazy. The things he was yelling shocked and confused me. I felt that he was going to hit me. I knew that he had hit his ex-girlfriend. I immediately left the room because I thought for sure that he was going to hit me. Ken closely followed me out into the living room, where my roommate was standing. Ken then stood over me, again with the same threatening expression, and his finger in my face. He continued cursing at me. He called me a "classless bitch," a "slut," a "little whore who turns tricks," and many other degrading things. Ken told me that he "had more class than I ever would." I then asked him why he had tried to make out with me (his friend's girlfriend.) He screamed that I was a "little whore if I was going to hold that against him to break up his friendship with Pat."

My roommate was standing with me, she saw and heard Ken's rampage. Some of Ken's housemates who were in a back room heard also. They are Evan Dienstag and Kristin [Gillis]. Ken continued to scream profanities at me for what seemed like forever. I was in shock. I couldn't move. This situation between Ken and I was not a heated argument. I could hardly get a word in edgewise. The only things I said were "Why did you come on to me Friday night?" and "Why are you being so mean?"

I am not an emotionally weak person. However, Ken's yelling, name calling, lies, and irrational behavior upset me so much that I started crying uncontrollably. I couldn't catch my breath. All the while Ken continued to curse at me. He told me that if I need an inhaler that they sell inhalers for "fucking asthmatics like (me)." My roommate grabbed me and drove me home. I was shaking and crying for hours afterwards. I had not done anything to Ken that would provoke or deserve such abuse. I told my boyfriend, Pat, what Ken had done to me. Pat and I heard Ken curse out his own mother in a similar fashion. I couldn't sleep that night. The next afternoon, Pat and I went to the apartment where Ken and Pat are housemates. Pat confronted Ken as I sat on the couch by the door. The noise level escalated, but there was no physical violence. Ken told Pat that I was a "whore," "loser," and " a bitch." At this time I started crying and shaking again. Then Ken's lies got worse. He claimed that on Sunday when I talked to him about the seventy dollars, I had pounded my way into his room and that I had struck him. This is not true. I know that Ken

*did not directly threaten me, but, he is very cunning. Ken
only does things when he thinks he won't get caught. He
is very good at not getting caught. Ken has an extremely
high temper. He already has a restraining order pre-
venting him from coming near Santa Cruz Residence
Halls at UCSB, where he once lived. He was put out of
the dorms because he got in a fight with another student
and beat him so severely that the student had to go to
the hospital. I feel in my heart of hearts that Ken will
abuse me again. Whether it be physical or verbal, I don't
know. However, verbal abuse hurts just as much, if not
more than physical violences. I am scared of Ken. My
roommates are afraid as well. Ken has a history of abu-
sive and irrational behavior. I don't want Ken coming
near me or my apartment.*

*I want a restraining order so Ken will not come near
me and hurt me again. I want to be able to stop Ken
before he does anything just as harmful or worse to me.*

In his defense, Kenny Kimes sent a four-page reply alleging Grammer to be his spurned would-be lover. The response was drafted by a Las Vegas attorney, John Rogers,
who, Kenny claimed, billed him $300 for his services. He
also testified that a Las Vegas secretarial service had
charged him $150 for typing not only his response but that
of four of his housemates who all seemed to support him
with similar affidavits. There was also a thirty-dollar charge
for the services of a notary public. Kenny attempted, but
failed, to get the "expenses" awarded to him in court.
Grammer had two supporting affidavits of her own to buttress her claims.

The responses of Kenny's housemates raise suspicions.
All were typed on the same word-processing machine, with
their signatures notarized in Las Vegas, rather than somewhere near UCSB. This means that Kenny would have had
to convince all four of his roommates to fly or drive from
Santa Barbara to Las Vegas in order to legally sign the documents in front of notary public Nanette O. Wetkowski, who
signed off on them. (A checking account in that name would

later be used to fraudulently purchase the Lincoln Town Car in Utah.)

The documents were also witnessed on a weekday, when classes at UCSB were being held. If Kenny managed to somehow have a Nevada notary put her official stamp on the papers with the documents already signed, he would have been getting a quick education on how to con the courts, previewing his apparent Irene Silverman deed-to-the-house scam by three years. In addition, all responses of the four have virtually the same phrases, as if written by the same person. However, some of the signatures do not seem to match the signature of the same students who signed the apartment lease, suggesting forgery (*see* Exhibit C). At one point, the name of a participant in an affadavit is spelled two different ways. Finally, there is no listing for a notary public by the name of Nanette Wetkowski, or an attorney by the name of John Rogers in Las Vegas. (Repeated calls to Kenny's housemates by the author asking for an explanation of the probable phony affadavits were not returned.)

Kenny's own sworn statement was certainly fanciful, but written more in the style of a fourteen-year-old than a twenty-year-old college student, bespeaking an arrested development. He claimed Grammer had come on to him and said, "Ken, you know you are the one that I really want and how come you have never tried to kiss me?" Kenny also stated that Grammer struck him on the chest "with a clenched fist." He then wrote, "She ran out of the room screaming, 'I am going to tell Pat [her boyfriend] that you wanted to kiss me!' " At one point Kenny says that Grammer "began pulling out her hair with both hands and started screaming at the top of her lungs for no reason in an extremely psychotic manner."

Grammer got a temporary restraining order against Kenny in early November, but claimed in court that he had telephoned her roommate, Lauren Schmalbach, on November 16 and threatened her the day before the scheduled court hearing. Grammer said Kenny warned her not to testify against him, thus violating the Santa Barbara sheriff's restraint command. The next day, November 17, 1995, Judge Thomas R. Adams declared a permanent mutual restraining order with both Grammer and Kenny not allowed to "threaten, strike, telephone, follow or block each other's movements in public places." However Grammer pursued Kenny's November 16 threat, asking for and getting another court date in January 1996. This brought Sante into the fray. She wrote a two-page, single-spaced letter of more than 1000 words to Judge Adams on January 9, 1996, telling him, "I have rushed here from the Bahamas to clear up this matter . . ."

Sante's missive began by complimenting the judge, and acting as if Kenny had won the November 17 hearing, adding that "My son and his roommates have now been the victims of harassment by Ms. Grammer for months, which has adversely affected their studies and interfered with the quiet enjoyment of their otherwise peaceful home . . . Ms Grammer, ignoring the court's final order, is pursuing the November 16 charge and has begun to harass the household of Mr. Kimes and his roommates again by making telephone calls again on January 4, 1996. She called the residence and began accusing them of impounding her bicycle."

Sante supported her letter with "affidavits" from three of Kenny's housemates, who all accused Grammer of continuing to harass her son. In this case, the documents were not only unwitnessed, they were unsigned. Kenny's mom did sign her own memorandum and, perhaps, unwittingly displaying a wicked sense of humor for puns. At the end of her note to Judge Adams, she wrote yet another alias, "Sante Khan" (*see* Exhibit D).

It's unclear from the Santa Barbara court papers if any further actions were ever taken against Kenny.

Sante's son never completed college, dropping out shortly after his court battle with Carrie Louise Grammer. The couple who befriended him when he was booted from his dorm for fighting, Trish and Alan Kadje, cautioned Kenny about leaving school and going off on a journey with his mom.

"No, I have to listen and do what my mother wants," Trish said he told her.

"Kenny, one of these days I'm probably going to have

to come and visit you in prison,'' the Santa Barbara cop warned him. He didn't tell Kenny of the chilling statement his mother had once made to him.

"Alan, you don't really know who I am,'' Sante said to Alan Kadje. "I'm not a very nice person.''

PART FOUR

We're facing a new type of criminal today who kills for kicks. People who are bored with life and have no discipline from without go along for kicks, until they must try the supreme kick, to kill another human being.

Erle Stanley Gardner

Chapter Fourteen

Journeys of Death

The Commonwealth of the Bahamas, a nation archipelago of some 700 islands, is just fifty miles off the coast of Florida. In addition to fine white-sand beaches, good snorkeling, and legalized gambling, the country claims to be able to offer Americans "the secrecy of a Swiss bank account with none of the disadvantages," according to one tourism document. The Bahamas' nearness to the U.S., its boast that the people speak English and the banks offer lower fees, are all considered pluses. There is no chance of the devaluation of your money, as in, for example, Mexico. The Bahamian dollar is also pegged to the U.S. dollar at par.

There are 350 different banks in the Bahamas for a populace of fewer than 200,000, primarily in its capital, Nassau, and on the second most-populated island, Freeport. Besides secrecy, a Bahamian bank account offers foreign visitors the privilege of not having to pay taxes on their dividends and interest payments. Royalties, capital gains, or an inheritance also go unlevied.

"The Bahamas are so close to the U.S. that it is possible to fly from New York or other major East Coast cities to Nassau, make transactions in person, and fly home on the same day," promises one Bahamian banking brochure.

Sources close to the Kimes family claim that Kenneth Kimes may have established as many as three "International Business Corporation" accounts, known as IBCs, in the Bahamas. Police sources suspect that decades of skimming cash from his motels had given him several million dollars that needed to be hidden, not only from Sante, but also from the Internal Revenue Service. An IBC account requires ''a minimum of documents and affords one a very high degree of confidentiality'' advertises one Bahamas bank.

When Ken Kimes died in 1994, sources believe that Sante could no longer legally remove funds from the Kimeses' Bahama Islands accounts. She continued to withdraw small amounts, they hypothesize, using forged signatures, until she was eventually detected. The man who discovered Sante's banking scam, the same sources say, probably paid with his life.

Sayed Bilal Ahmed, a native of the Arab emirate state of Bahrain, was both a vice president of the First Cayman Bank on Grand Cayman Island and an auditor of the Gulf Union Bank in Nassau. The disarming, friendly fifty-five-year-old led a jet-set life, island-hopping among several Caribbean nations. He was an expert on offshore banking law. In February 1996, less than a month after Kenny's court battle with Carrie Louise Grammer, he was spotted by a local auto dealer in Georgetown, the Caymans' capital, with Sante and Kenny.

''Although I was good friends with Ahmed, I did not want to intrude because it looked like a [banker-client] meeting,'' the owner of the car lot, Raafat Khalil, later told Reuters.

Khalil said he remembered Kenny and the Liz Taylor lookalike when he saw their picture on television two years later. By that time, Ahmed had been named a missing person.

''Then it came back to me. It was her and and they most certainly knew Ahmed well when he disappeared,'' said Khalil.

Police sources theorize that Ahmed soon found irregularities in one or more of the Kimeses' Bahamas accounts and wanted an explanation. Sante and Kenny told him they could explain everything and next used a ploy—establishing a Caribbean Internet business with Ahmed as a favored partner—to get him alone. Isolating the banker, Sante and Kenny left Grand Cayman on a flight with Ahmed that stopped in Miami on its way to Nassau on September 5, 1996. Within hours after arriving, Ahmed evaporated into a wet Nassau night and was never seen again. His luggage at the Radisson Cable Beach hotel, where he checked in on September 5, also vanished. A reservation for three had been made by Ahmed in the Radisson's restaurant but nobody showed. The hotel is less than a mile from Sante's Bahamas beach home.

The Police Superintendent of the Commonwealth of the Bahamas, Douglas Hanna, continues to list Sante as his chief suspect in the vanishing. He says his police force can't wait to talk to her.

"We'd very much like to speak to [Sante Kimes]," Hanna said. "The missing man [Ahmed] was at the house where the Kimeses were staying in Nassau around the fifth or sixth of September, which was the time he was reported missing. Once Mrs. Kimes knew we were inquiring about her she couldn't be found."

After Ahmed was reported missing, with the Bahamian police alerted to lookout for her at the airport, Sante was afraid to go back to Nassau. She believed she could be arrested if she spent any serious time on Bahamian soil. But there was money in several Nassau banks in the Kimes name—lots of it. She tried to scam her way back into the country, and get a cash transfusion by sending in a surrogate.

On May 12, 1997, a middle-aged woman by the name of Donna Frances Lawson walked into a Miami courthouse late in the afternoon and asked for a passport, saying she wanted to travel to the Commonwealth of the Bahamas. The clerk thought her request strange because the Bahamas doesn't usually require a passport for U. S. citizens. The woman also had identification that showed a photo of a woman who was twenty years younger. She was arrested and, when interrogated, immediately came clean.

She told the State Department's Diplomatic Security Service agents that she was Sante Kimes' maid. Sante had stolen the ID papers from her daughter, Lawson claimed. Ken and Sante had then sent her to Miami to get a passport, so she could travel to the Bahamas "to clean Mrs. Kimes' house on Cable Beach.'' While the Feds didn't buy the ''getting-a-passport-to-clean-a-house'' tale, they certainly wanted to speak with Sante about the missing Bahamian banker, Sayed Bilal Ahmed.

Donna Lawson was more than willing to blab to the feds on the whereabouts of her employer's residence. Sante was hiding out in a small one-bedroom flat at a downtown Fort Lauderdale apartment-motel called the Blue Bell, which she was renting furnished for $600 a month.

With Lawson looking for leniency by leading the way to Sante Kimes, six diplomatic service agents rushed to the motel, guns drawn. Pushing open the door, the feds rushed in only to find open suitcases with clothes spilling out of them, blank legal forms lying on the kitchen table next to half-eaten food, dishes in the sink, several wigs, but no mother and son.

''It was like someone had just walked out the door,'' special agent Walter B. Deering remembered. ''She left ten minutes before we got there. And she was gone. Simply gone.''

Belen Papp, the manager of the motel, believed Sante was tipped off.

''She knew they were coming,'' Papp claimed in an interview with the Fort Lauderdale *Sun Sentinel*. ''So she went to the back of the building to hide.''

Deering said later that the ''maid'' didn't know that Sante was being sought in Ahmed's disappearance. Donna Lawson's revised story was that Sante had told her she was avoiding a subpoena in a civil matter.

''The woman we arrested appeared to be a pawn. We wanted the real kingpin,'' said agent Deering.

Frustrated that she couldn't get back into the Bahamas to grab more money out of big Ken's bank accounts, Sante and Ken became grifting whirlwinds during their 1997 stay in Florida.

Prior to the passport scam attempt, Sante had strolled into a Fort Lauderdale motor vehicle bureau in April, used a fake name, and received a new state ID card under the name of her so-called ''maid,'' Donna Frances Lawson. She also gave a fictitious address and a new birthdate—July 11, 1943.

On May 20, 1997, Sante was spotted on aisle six of the Federal Discount Store in downtown Miami by plainclothes detective Jose Alfonso. He said later that the woman ''looked like Liz Taylor with her big black hair, black bell-bottom trousers, and a sleazy fishnet blouse.''

Tagging along with her was a young man in shorts and sneakers who Miami police said was Kenny.

Detective Alfonso watched Sante swipe several tubes of Revlon lipstick, slit their blister-packs with her long finger-nails in front of a store clerk while she misdirected his eyes, and slip the nineteen dollars' worth of the cosmetics into her purse. The cop then moved in, flashed his badge, and asked to look into her handbag. Sante was ready. She quickly went into action, jumping up and onto the police plainsclothesman, and surprised him with her shouts.

''He's assaulting me! He's robbing me! He's assaulting me!'' she yelled.

That gave Kenny the excuse he needed to run to his mom's rescue and attempt to remove her from the cop's grasp. When her son was by her side, Sante, in a move worthy of an NFL quarterback, pitched him the large pock-etbook, with Kenny—who surely must have wished he was back in college that day—catching it on the run. Momen-tarily confused, Alfonso saw the two flee the store. Wit-nesses soon pointed the way to a nearby five-and-dime emporium, where the cop caught up to the pair. Since Kenny still had the purse, the detective tackled him, allowing Sante to slip out through the rear of the store while the two men struggled. After overpowering and cuffing him, he took him to the nearest police precinct.

Kenny had been taught well. He at first refused to even speak, and would not confirm the name in his wallet. The cops sent out a warrant for the escapee, ''Donna Frances Lawson,'' the name that was under the picture of Sante in the ID from the recovered bag. Kenny was charged with ''strong arm robbery, resisting arrest, battery on a police officer, and obstructing an arrest of a 'disguised' person.'' He gave the cops a fake address and a phony Social Security number. A lawyer soon showed up at Miami police head-quarters, getting Kenny out of jail on bond with a $10,000 check.

"I had a gut instinct there was more to these people," Jose Alfonso would tell the *Miami Herald* a little more than a year later. "She was twenty years too old for the outfit and hidden under two inches of makeup. And nobody invokes their rights to remain silent over a Revlon robbery."

After sending out the warrant for the arrest of "Donna Frances Lawson," the Miami cops found that a person operating under that name, but resembling Sante, was also wanted for a recent auto theft. A "Donna Lawson" had failed to return a rental car (a variation of Sante's usual new-car, test-drive scam) that had been checked out on a two-day contract on February 3, 1997. Daytona Beach police in Volusia County wanted to talk to her about the missing car. However, Sante and Ken were on the move yet again, headed back to California in their quest to gain more chunks of big Ken's fortune.

Like so many of their marks, David Kazdin had met Sante and Papa Kimes in a Las Vegas casino during the late 1970s. The fact that he ran a business from his suburban Los Angeles home in the San Fernando Valley, copying medical documents, was enough said. Sante quickly befriended him.

Over the years, big Ken had given Kazdin enough real estate advice for the businessman to be obligated. In 1992, Ken Kimes leaned on his friend for a favor. He told Kazdin he needed to "temporarily transfer" the deed to the house on Geronimo Way in Las Vegas and put it in his name. It was a small business favor, Ken explained. Kazdin thought it was a pretty strange request. But, what could he lose, he figured? Besides he had little choice. He felt indebted to Papa Kimes.

With big Ken dead, and Sante and Kenny having bad luck in the Bahamas, not to mention the unfortunate hijinks in Miami where one newspaper had ridiculed Sante by calling her "the Revlon bandit," Sante made another try for a big score. According to South Florida police sources, Sante and Kenny showed up at West Palm Beach-based Ocwen Financial Corporation in 1997. Its subsidiary, Ocwen Federal Savings Bank, advertised itself as an "established leader in the acquisition of troubled real-estate loans."

Sante, who by now may have had more blank legal forms than the thrift itself, talked a loan officer into giving her a $280,000 second mortgage on the house in the name of David Kazdin. Los Angeles detective David English says the loan documents were "fraudulently notarized." The notary public who had made the transfer was Nanette O. Wetkowski. Police believe Sante took between $100,000 and $150,000 of the cash and deposited it in an offshore Caribbean financial firm, the Bank of Antigua, attempting to hide the money. Part of the cash would be used to retain her New York lawyers less than a year later.

According to a friend of Kazdin's in Los Angeles, Kazdin was "apoplectic" when he got the monthly coupon payment book from the Florida bank. He had dinner with an insurance adjustor who knew Sante Kimes well and, over a steak, his friend gave him some straight advice.

"David, you're in danger if you pursue this. She can kill you," he was told.

Kazdin didn't believe him at first. He went ahead and called Sante to protest the mortgage taken out in his name and told her to get his name off the deed or he was going to the police. Sante was soothing and compliant but, still, it was a long, bizarre conversation. After talking for more than an hour with her, he told his lawyer, Phil Eaton, what he thought of the wife of Ken Kimes.

"This woman is crazy. She'll do anything," he said.

Sante took Kazdin's name off the mortgage and put it in the name of Robert McCarren aka Frank McCarren, an indigent Las Vegas man she had befriended. McCarren lived in a homeless shelter. She immediately made McCarren take out the maximum fire-prevention insurance one could buy from the Fireman's Fund Insurance Company. On January 31, just two weeks after the policy was approved by the insurer, the Geronimo Way house burned to the ground. A fire-department dog, trained to sniff out possible arson, determined that all fourteen rooms of the house had been soaked with gasoline, probably by someone walking backward while pouring it. Las Vegas fire investigator Mike Patterson's first thought was the Kimes family.

"But," said Patterson, "I couldn't find hair nor hide of them."

Patterson's department notified Fireman's Fund Insurance of their belief that the blaze on Geronimo Way had been deliberately set. An investigator for the company arranged to meet with McCarren and thought it strange that the "homeowner" would only agree to meet with him in the lobby of a hotel next to the Los Angeles International Airport.

According to the LAPD, McCarren got through the interview smoothly at first. He even managed to give them a bank-account number where Fireman's Fund could wire the money (it was Sante's account) to pay for the claim. McCarren had no choice but to try and convince the investigator. Reprising a bad habit, Sante and Kenny had been keeping him locked up and enslaved in their Bel Air house for weeks, telling anyone who asked about him that he was her "mute valet." As McCarren spun his tale, the mother and her son sat on a sofa, almost within touching distance. They sipped tea, and listened to his every word.

McCarren, who later escaped from Sante's custody in a breakout similar to some of the Mexican maids a dozen years earlier, told police that Sante and Kenny had rehearsed him for days prior to his meeting with Fireman's Fund. When he made a mistake in the practice sessions, he testified to the L.A. cops, Sante would beat or slap him.

"Mrs. Kimes is an incredible manipulator and the most controlling woman I've ever seen," a Fireman's Fund investigator would say later. "She has controlled and intimidated McCarren, as she has tried to control everyone she's ever known."

The insurance company refused to pay on the Geronimo Way claim. And David Kazdin was still complaining about the dunning notices he was getting from Florida, making noises as if he finally was going to do something about it.

Just after ten in the morning on Saturday, March 14, 1998, David Kazdin's bullet-riddled body was found by a

"Dumpster diver" looking for recyclables. He had been shot through the head and in other parts of the body with a .22 pistol.

Kazdin's remains were found at 9814 Belford Avenue, a short street in Los Angeles near the airport, and less than two miles from The Great Western Forum sports arena. It is an area Sante undoubtedly knew well. The street is within blocks of where Sante's mother—and possibly Sante herself—had worked as a prostitute. Police believe it took a strong man to lift the dead weight of the sixty-three-year-old Kazdin, and pitch him into the trash receptacle.

The night David Kazdin was killed, Sante and Kenny were living in a rental home nearby, under eviction orders for their strange behavior, but holed up in half of the luxurious house at 3221 Elvido Drive halfway up a Bel Air hillside. They left town shortly after the photocopy executive's death, behind the wheel of their scammed-with-a-bum-check green Lincoln Town Car, first to Las Vegas, then grifting their way back to Florida for another attempt at getting more of Ken's money out of the Bahamas.

As soon as they sped out of the City of Angels, the other occupant of the house, Jill Gardner, began checking out the rooms of the Bel Air home. She went into the garage and noticed a box they had left behind. Gardner, who had begun carrying a gun on her person because of suspicions about Kenny and Sante's activities, opened the box. Inside was David Kazdin's passport, driver's license, and, as Gardner later told the LAPD, "everything." She had read of Kazdin's demise in the newspapers and she knew something, as she put it, "was very, very wrong."

As usual, the mother and her son were two steps ahead, grifting their way back across America, headed for the Sunshine State.

When Sante fled Florida in 1997, she left behind an thirteen-year-old motor home Ken Kimes had owned for years. Kenny had hidden the RV between a row of horse vans in the equestrian area of Wellington, a gated horsey playground for society types near Palm Beach. Wellington was most famous for hosting Prince Charles and his young bride, Diana, in 1985. In those happier days, Charles displayed his polo skills while Di cheered him on. During April 1998 Sante rented a villa inside the Wellington enclosure using her old alias, Sandra Walker.

One of Sante and Kenny's first Florida scams that spring was to buy a new $83,000, thirty-six-foot-long Holiday Rambler motor home, from Dixie Motors in Hammond, Louisiana, a community of 15,000, midway between New Orleans and Baton Rouge. Dixie was a Lincoln-Mercury dealer with a motor-home lot next door. Sante had dropped by on the way to Florida and, using the familiar name Nannette O. Wetkowski, got a car salesman salivating by posing as a little old lady willing to pay the full list price if they would only take the 1997 green Lincoln off her hands and then, maybe, she would like an RV for her son. According to Palm Beach police sources, it was Sante Kimes at her grifting best.

When Sante got to Florida, she used the Nanette O. Wetkowski name when she phoned Dixie Motors again, reminding them who she was and asking them to have someone drive the Holiday Rambler home-on-wheels to the posh Ritz-Carlton Hotel in Manalapan, a lush barrier island community next to Palm Beach. The recreational vehicle dealer told her it would expect a certified check. No problem, Sante responded. She certainly had a certified-check rubber stamp among her collection of conning tools, as well as any other documentation they needed.

On May 30, when the driver arrived at the Ritz-Carlton with the motor home, Sante was there to greet him, using yet another alias. She told the Dixie Motors courier that she was a representative of the buyer, who was inside the hotel and didn't wish to be disturbed. Using misdirection, as confidently as if she were a three-card-monte hustler, Sante began to express doubts about the motor home's soundness, threatening not to pay. She told her "servant," whom Sante called Jose, to go for a test drive with the Louisiana car dealer's employee. While he was diverted, Sante took the sales documents and disappeared into the hotel, returning five minutes later with two "certified" checks totaling $70,000. (The dealer had given her a $13,000 trade-in allowance on the old RV.) The relieved messenger, who had thought for a moment that he might have had to go home with a busted deal, didn't examine the two checks all that closely.

The first check, for $7,000, bore the signature of one of Sante's favorite puns, her humorous S.A. Kahn moniker, the same name she used trying to butter up Kenny's judge back in Santa Barbara.. The $63,000 check was signed by a L. M. Carpaneto, a Los Angeles man who had reported his checkbook and wallet stolen in Las Vegas just a few weeks before.

Dixie Motors realized that the checks were no good a few days later, and called the Palm Beach police immediately. A cop finally found the Holiday Rambler on June 20, three weeks after the Louisiana dealer blew the whistle. Sante had stashed the vehicle in the same equestrian area of Wellington in which she had hidden the older motor home a year before. The vehicle's serial numbers had been filed off, forcing the police to have to confirm the Holiday Rambler as the stolen vehicle by checking the digits on its propane tank and water heater.

"If you're bold enough and have most of your ducks in a row, if you're playing the part good, you can get almost anyone to take you at face value," concluded Tom Clark, a local detective who helped find the house-on-wheels.

Meanwhile, Sante, displaying a woman's prerogative, had decided to alter her game plan. She had heard of a rich old lady in Manhattan who seemed so ripe for the plucking she couldn't resist. Sante and Kenny—and his new friend, Jose Antonio Alvarez—jumped back in the green Lincoln and headed up north on Interstate 95 for New York, New York.

Chapter Fifteen

End Game

Manhattan's marvelous summer of 1998 finally ended. The first cool nights delighted those New Yorkers who liked to sleep with the window open. Mel Sachs' handsomely paid mouth was still moving, no matter what season the case had entered, speaking out on the Kimeses' innocence to anyone who would listen. The Jimmy Hoffa lookalike, with his straight, slicked-back gray hair, seemed excited just to be a legal servant to Kenny and Sante. He told one of his audiences: "It isn't the case of the century, it's the case of the millennium! It's the case of a lifetime!"

Obfuscating freely, he began to speak in staccato bursts about the vanished Sayed Bilal Ahmed, saying, "There are people who would benefit from this banker, not the Kimeses. The Kimeses aren't considered suspects in that case. We're going to show to the American public who really are involved in these disappearances. This can happen to anyone. We have to be sure justice prevails here and the individuals who are involved here are brought to justice—not the Kimeses."

When a questioner on an ABC TV Internet press conference reminded him that a judge once called Sante "the pure essence of evil," Sachs was quick to refute the charge. "They are not career criminals. In regards to the son, Kenny Kimes, he does not have a criminal record at all and I have all the criminal records from Florida. There was an incident involved and what happened in that incident is nothing at all. He's not a career criminal. He's not a criminal at all.

The representation that was made to the public is false. Sante is not a criminal. She had one case that involved the taking of property. The genesis of the case involving involuntary servitude was a civil case where an attorney who represented the workers of the Kimeses tried to obtain money from the Kimes.

"They used the courts to get money from them. They then went to another court and brought charges of involuntary servitude. When the facts come out you'll find out she isn't a career criminal. You have to look at the entire case and not just the remarks of a judge. You have to look at the entire transcript.

"Her [Sante's] background, which may not be a sterling background—and that might disturb you—yet there isn't anything showing that she would be involved with murder.The things that Sante Kimes has done in the past are not anything like what she's been accused of now. Sante and Kenny Kimes are not career criminals and I urge you to give them fair treatment. They are two human beings who are being condemned."

His audience had to be impressed. With the pedantic Mel Sachs one could begin to believe that if only Marv Albert and Bill Clinton had been his clients, one of them would be asked to judge a teen beauty pageant while the other would be chosen as the competition's master of ceremonies.

By early September, Sachs had invited the acerbic *New York Post* columnist Cindy Adams to his office for a one-to-one chat with Sante. Adams didn't get any major revelations from Mrs. Kimes—that was to be expected with the phone tapped—except maybe Sante's claim that she had lost eighteen pounds on the Rikers Island cuisine, saying she couldn't sleep and had no appetite. One tabloid wag wondered out loud if the public might like a page of recipes headlined "Ma Kimes' Quick Loss Prison Diet."

"I cannot bear this for my child," Sante whimpered to the city's proclaimed diva of dish. "Every mother in the world can share my pain."

Sante's hyperboles from her cell knew no bounds. To her, Kenny was a mother's dream come true.

"He [Kenny] is everything any mother would want,"

Sante sobbed, trying to con all of New York through Cindy Adams' widely read column. "A loving, caring, wonderful son—with such goodness. Even in his school days, he brought me only happiness. He was fun, loving, never a fight, never a problem, always getting along with people.

"When my husband died, [Kenny] left college to care for me. He was an honor student. He worked at a hospice for the terminally ill."

Sante told Adams all she cared about was Kenny.

"Even if he is grown, he is still to me my son. He has never done anything criminal. Not in the past, not now. I am innocent of this as well, but my heart goes out to [Kenny]. I don't know if he's all right, if he's well, is he eating, is he getting enough sleep . . ."

Sante kept emoting to Cindy Adams until her captors took the phone away and hung up on the columnist. After the interview, Sachs pointed the finger at the man the press had labeled "the third suspect," the Hispanic man who had been named by the police, Jose Antonio Alvarez.

"When the individual, Jose Antonio Alvarez is located, it will clearly show that Sante and Kenneth Kimes had absolutely nothing to do with the disappearance of Irene Silverman," Sachs declared.

NYPD commissioner Howard Safir was also looking for Alvarez. He had Sante well pegged by now.

"It is not unusual for [the Kimeses] to attach themselves to people who are either unemployed or down on their luck and utilize them," Safir said.

Jose Antonio Alvarez—to whom at least one newspaper would initially ascribe the first name of Jesus—was a twenty-four-year-old Cuban who had immigrated legally to America in 1993. Alvarez had no arrest record, just a pile of old debts that he wanted to pay. He lived in a trailer park with his mother in Belle Glade, Florida, thirty-five miles southwest of Palm Beach. He often worked in the tony resort town, taking jobs as a short-order cook in fast-food joints, a fate that was at least easier than the seasonal labor he found in the sugar-cane fields of south-central Florida.

Belle Glade, a town of nearly 15,000 near the shores of

Lake Okeechobee, was a forlorn fishing village for bass anglers who camped on the cheap just outside town. The black and Hispanic immigrant residents, who sweated in the low-paying agricultural jobs next to the misnamed community, were beset with diseases caused by disease-carrying mosquitoes. Belle Glade's other employment opportunity was the Glades Correctional Center, a state prison. The municipality had the highest AIDS rate in the state and the highest number of unwed births among teenagers. Since being leveled by a hurricane that killed 2000 locals in 1928, it had never really been rebuilt. The community did have one claim to fame—actress Demi Moore had recently been there filming the movie *Striptease*. Other than that, Belle Glade was a good place to say you were *from* rather than claiming citizenry of the poverty-stricken place.

So, on May 14, 1998, when Kenny Kimes offered Alvarez a chance to be his personal manservant, hinting that he was very, very rich, the Cuban emigre leaped at the job offer. He had never met a millionaire, let alone worked for one. And a trip to the Big Apple—he had only seen New York on television and in the movies. Yes, he would be happy to chauffeur them around in their big green Lincoln. Sante's Spanish wasn't Cuban Spanish, but he could communicate with Mama Kimes in his first language while he continued to perfect his English.

On June 10, Alvarez was behind the wheel with Kenny at his side, and Sante grandly alone in the rear seat as they began their final 1200-mile, two-day journey to America's largest city. The Cuban youth thought the mother and son were a strange combination, but maybe that was how millionaires were supposed to behave. On the final day of their trip, Sante had insisted they stay overnight in New Jersey. They were so close, the sugar-cane laborer could see the twin towers jutting up over lower Manhattan.

The next day, heading into the city, he thought some of Kenny's remarks were pretty spooky. He would later tell the NYPD that Kenny had looked at a swampy area just before Jersey City and said, almost wistfully, to no one in particular, "That would be a great place to hide a body."

*   *   *

It did appear to be a good disposal site. Certainly, the New York cops agreed. When the NYPD finally located Jose Alvarez in late August 1998 and interrogated him, they had him point out where Kenny had made the remark. The Cuban, for his part, claimed that he had deserted the two on June 22, long before Irene Silverman's disappearance.

"They were a bit strange, so I left," he told New York's WNBC in an interview.

Part of his story didn't ring true. Even though he had been caught on the surveillance camera inside Irene's East 65th Street mansion, and admitted staying there, Alvarez claimed he had never laid eyes on the vanished widow. He declined to answer other questions, telling the press he was under police orders not to talk.

"Detectives have forbidden me to speak about it. My lawyers have done the same," said the potentially important witness to the *Daily News*. He had a right to be upset. Sante hadn't paid him for his services and probably never would. Because of the Kimeses he was on the run from reporters, hiding out in Miami, and back to working as a bus boy.

The New York cops made one last try to find Irene, fanning out over the area where Alvarez said Kenny had made the "hide-a-body" remark. The site was a little larger than a football field, and just north of Saint Peter's Cemetery, between Jersey City and the Meadowlands sports complex in New Jersey. It was a barren spot, full of tall weeds, old mattresses, and parts of abandoned cars—a good place to bury a body you didn't want found. More than twenty officers in white uniforms, looking like astronauts with their head gear off, fanned out. They had dogs on leashes trained to sniff and discover decomposing corpses. After two days and and a total of eighteen hours searching for Irene, they found some bones. They were chicken bones. They took their weed whackers and their shovels and went home. It would be the last search they would make for the missing widow's body.

Mel Sachs made a final stab at springing Kenny and Sante. On September 4, 1998, appearing before a more sympathetic justice, New York Criminal Court Judge Walter

Tingling, he got the jurist to warn prosecutor Carmen Morales that she must make a serious charge by the end of September or he would consider bail for the two grifters.

Tingling warned Morales that the city's continuing to keep them in jail on a credit-card-fraud charge and a warrant from Utah without bail was a "weak reason." If Utah didn't extradite the two by September 30, he said he would dismiss the credit-card fraud and offer them bail. Sachs was exultant.

"This would also totally weaken the prosecution's forgery case against them and their ability to further hold them in preventive detention. [Prosecutors] have only the barest, weakest circumstantial case," Sachs said.

On September 18, trying to succeed at getting bail where Sachs had failed, Jose Muniz also made a final run at freeing Sante and Kenny before Acting Manhattan Supreme Court Justice Herbert Altman, pulling out all the stops. This time, he claimed Sante was a genuine hero who had been marked for death by a Panamanian drug gang because she had saved the life of a prosecutor who had put the narcotics smugglers in jail.

"She is responsible for saving the life of a U.S. attorney," Muniz blustered. "That is why she used aliases. My client was involved with issues of national security where it was important and prudent for her to protect her from those threats and to protect her son."

Howard Zlotnick, of the U.S. Attorney's office in Las Vegas, said that Sante's story was news to him. He had never heard of any such plot.

Muniz said he got the revelation from Sante's former lawyer. He wouldn't name him and admitted he didn't know the name of the U.S. attorney whose life his client had saved. Justice Altman was not impressed. He continued the court's no-bail ruling until at least October 22.

"We're innocent. Pray for us. All we want is justice. My son is wonderful. We're innocent," Sante spouted to her favorite courtroom sketch artist, Jane Rosenberg, as she was being led away. The repetitive "we're innocent" lines were becoming her mantra.

*   *   *

On December 16, 1998, Sante Kimes and her son Kenny were indicted on eighty-four counts of murder, burglary, grand theft, robbery, and forgery. If convicted of every charge, the maximum penalty they will receive would be in the words of the prosecution, "one hundred thirty-one years to life."

A grand jury had heard from seventy witnesses, including Jose Alvarez and Stan Patterson, both of whom had testified against them in exchange for immunity. The Nevada cowboy told the jurors that Sante had ordered him to go into Irene's building and "fire the employees, evict the tenants, change the locks, and take over the building."

By now, Jose Muniz had quit the case, partly because of his clients' inability to get their hands on a dwindling reserve of money. It was left to Mel Sachs to address the press alone, using the now-familiar phrase that the indictments were based on "speculation, innuendo, and unfounded rumors."

"There is no proof Mrs. Silverman is even dead," he claimed.

Police admitted that they faced a difficult journey in convicting Sante and Kenny of murder. They still were without a confession, and had found no physical evidence that Irene was harmed or dead.

"It's difficult to confirm a death in the absence of a coroner's statement or medical testimony," cautioned Barry Schreiber, a deputy district attorney in Brooklyn.

A trial expected to take place in the latter half of 1999 would push a jury to the limit if a murder conviction were sought without either element, legal sources said.

"It's nice to have a body," said the silver-haired D.A. Bob Morgenthau. "But we would never want to send the message that all you have to do is hide the body and you get off scot-free."

Then, showing as much emotion as he ever had, Morganthau, whom the press was now calling "Morgy," looked over his oversized glasses and stated, "These are vicious, cold-blooded killers."

In Los Angeles, Brian Carr of the LAPD vowed to charge

Kenny and Sante with the murder of David Kazdin if New York failed to convict the pair.

"We have a much stronger case than New York," he said. He claimed there was a witness who had seen Kenny standing over Kazdin's body with a gun in his hand.

In court for their arraignment, Kenny and Sante said nothing. It was hard to read them. But if you had to, the best bet is that they were sifting through their thick file of scams and cons, looking for one that might be the key to their freedom. They continued to hold hands like lovers, until the judge ordered them to stop.

Epilogue

In one of the snapshots Ruth Tanis has of the close childhood friend she first knew as Sandy Chambers, there is a photo that shows a teen-aged Sante lying in a grassy field next to a newborn foal. The idyllic picture could be a scene from *National Velvet*, the film responsible for launching Elizabeth Taylor. I have stared at the image for hours, wondering what transformed a once-popular young girl with a solid future into a vicious thief, a confidence artist, a keeper of slaves, and an accused killer who chose to pass these traits on to her son.

Of course, a psychiatrist could come up with lots of reasons for Sante's deeds. A follower of Freud will tell you that Sante stole and forced servants to work without pay as a way to compensate for how deprived she felt with the cards of life she had been dealt. Her childhood, traveling from the dust bowl of Oklahoma to the streets of Los Angeles, taught her never to trust providence. What others had by right of birth—a sense of security and entitlement—was something she tasted briefly and then never again. If there were a devil's curse, a shrink will say, it was a feeling of unrelenting neediness that could never be fulfilled. She was never able to feel satisfied with either wealth or possessions.

Falling in with Ken Kimes, a rich hustler who shared a similar Depression background, helped to keep Sante's crimes penaltyfree for more than a decade. But, after his death, her security blanket was snatched away. Threatened with uncertainty and perhaps the fear of being destitute, her worst instincts took over.

People like Sante Kimes live their lives on the edge of perceived desperation, making all their decisions based on irrational needs and anger. They decide everything on a quick, emotional level, believing that everyone else has a free passage through life—a voyage denied to them. This gives them the excuse they use to lash out and express themselves through theft of property, and other, much more violent actions. Sante Kimes and her kind are a danger to all of us and yet the men and women responsible for our safety rarely act early enough to confine them. Though it is unlikely that Sante Kimes will ever see freedom again, her son Kenny—given his age—might eventually be released if other pending murder charges are not brought forward and successfully prosecuted. Her other son, Kent, claims he is estranged from Sante. He has done little to help his mother publicly and is staying far away from her legal struggles.

Children can betray a parent in many ways. Kenny's final attempt to break his mother's lifelong spell over him may be to make her responsible for the death of Irene Silverman. Certainly, Sante is also capable of cutting a deal at the expense of her son. The most ferocious animals often eat their young to survive. Their upcoming courtroom battle against the New York City legal system will be fascinating to watch evolve.

If you walk down the short block of East 65th Street in New York between Central Park and Madison Avenue today, Irene Silverman's mansion will look much the way it did before she vanished. The yellow tape is gone, the bloodstains on the sidewalk have long since disappeared, and the NYPD van with the watchful eyes inside has been driven away from its spot in front of house number twenty.

The carved stone god is still there, though, directly above the door. Squint your eyes as you stroll by, and you might imagine more woe than wry behind the faint smile curling from its full lips. The fierce face might beam again in revelry, you tell yourself, when total vengeance is wrought.

APPENDIXES

Appendix A

Partial List of Adult Crimes Charged to Sante Kimes

02-12-61	Sacramento, California	Petty theft
12-29-65	Los Angeles, California	Grand theft
12-30-65	Norwalk, California	Auto theft
01-03-66	Norwalk, California	Warrant for arrest issued
11-15-68	Glendale, California	Unspecified charge dismissed
11-25-68	Riverside, California	Grand theft
04-26-72	Santa Ana, California	Forged credit card, grand larceny, grand theft
08-10-72	Palm Springs, California	Grand theft
09-27-74	Newport Beach, California	Grand theft

02-08-80	Washington, D.C.	Grand larceny
08-03-85	La Jolla, California	Involuntary servitude (keeping slaves)
05-19-97	Miami, Florida	Shoplifting, strong-arm robbery
07-05-98	Cedar City, Utah	Forged check
07-31-98	New York, New York	Credit card fraud
12-16-98	New York, New York	Second-degree murder, robbery, burglary, grand larceny, forgery, and other charges

Appendix B

Partial List of Adult Crimes Charged to Kenny Kimes

05-19-98	Miami, Florida	Strong-arm robbery
07-31-98	New York, New York	Credit card fraud
12-26-98	New York, New York	Second-degree murder, robbery, burglary, grand larceny, forgery, and other charges

Appendix C

Names and Aliases Used by the Accused

Mrs. Kenneth K. Kimes aka Mrs. Ken Kimes aka Sante Kimes aka Shante Kimes aka Santee Kimes aka Shantee Kimes aka Sante Louise Singhrs aka Sante Singhres aka Sandra Singhrs aka Sandra Singrhres aka Sandra Singer aka Sondra Singer aka Sandra Chambers aka Mrs. Lee Powers aka Sandra Louise Powers aka Mrs. Edward Walker aka Mrs Eddy Walker aka Sandra Walker aka Sandy Kimes aka Sante Singres Kimes aka Sandra Louise Walker aka Louise Sante Walker aka Sante Khan aka S. A. Khan aka Sandra Louise Walker aka Louise Walker aka Marjorie Walker aka Santa Louisa Powers aka Sandra L. Singhers aka Sane Taj Singhrs, aka Sante Salligman aka Sandra Seligman aka Sandy Jacobson aka Santee Louise Walker aka Donna Frances Lawson aka Donna Lawson aka Eva Guerrero, and others.

* * *

Mr. Kenneth Kareem Kimes aka Kenneth Karam Kimes aka Ken Kimes aka Kenny Kimes aka Manny Guerrin aka Manuel Guerro aka Tony Tsoukas, and others.

Appendix D

Excerpted Sworn Deposition of Adela Sanchez in Her Lawsuit Against Sante Kimes on March 23rd, 1988

(The attorney for the plaintiff, Adela Sanchez, was Robert K. Merce, Esq., of Schutter, Playdon and Glickstein of Honolulu, Hawaii. The attorney for Sante Kimes was J. Mitchell Cobeaga, Esq., of Beckly, Singleton, De Lanoy, Jemison, and List of Las Vegas, Nevada. Ms. Sanchez's testimony was in Spanish and translated by interpreters Rebecca Munoz and Mirta Susana B. Hess.)

Q What happened when you told Mrs. Kimes that you wanted to return to Costa Mesa?
A She started hitting me, like slapping me with her hand.

Q What part of the house did this take place in?
A In the kitchen.

Q Were there any other times, other than the two that you described, when you were beaten

while you were staying at the house in Las Vegas?
A Yes.

Q *Tell us about when the other times occurred.*
A *Later, also, she hit me again.*

Q *What were you doing just before she hit you on this occasion?*
A *I don't remember.*

Q *Could you just tell us what happened to you?*
A *She started hitting me with some hangers.*

Q *You mean clothes hangers?*
A Yes.

Q *At that time did you have in mind anything that you had done to deserve a beating with coat hangers?*

   Mr. Cobeaga: I'm just going to interpose an objection to the use of the word beating. I believe she said she was struck with a coat hanger and we may be introducing semantics.

   The Witness: Would you repeat the question?

   By Mr. Merce:
Q *Did you have anything in mind that you thought you might have done wrong to prompt your being hit with the coat hanger?*

A It was because I also told her that I wanted to go back.

Q To Costa Mesa?
A Yes.

Q Could you describe the coat hanger that she used to strike you?
A First she took one made out of wood.

Q Where did she hit you with that?
A In my legs.

Q The front or the back of your legs?
A On the back.

Q Did she then use a different type of coat hanger?
A Yes.

Q Tell us about that.
A She took those made out of wire and she started hitting me with these.

Q Where did she hit you with the wire coat hanger?
A Also on my legs.

Q Did she hit you hard?
A Yes.

Q How long did she hit you with the coat hanger?
A Several times.

Q Do you know why she switched from hitting you with wooden coat hangers to the wire coat hangers?
A Because the wooden hangers were getting broken.

Q How did they break?
A They would get broken in the middle, in half.

Q When they came into contact with you?
A Yes.

Q Did Mrs. Kimes ever strike you on any other occasions?
A She would always slap me.

Mr. Cobeaga: I'm sorry, could I have your answer again?
The Witness: She would always slap me.

By Mr. Merce:
Q Did you ever talk to Mr. Kimes about the way that Mrs. Kimes was treating you?
A That day that she hit me with the hangers, he went to my room because he saw me crying.

Mr. Harding: Objection. I would ask that the answer be stricken as nonresponsive to the question that was posed. The question called for a yes or no.
Mr. Merce: Can I have the question read back?

(Record read as requested.)

By Mr. Merce:
Q On the day tht you were beaten with the wooden and wire coat hangers, did you ever talk to Mr. Kimes about the way that his wife Santee was treating you, yes or no?
A Yes.

Q Were you emotionally upset at that time or not?
A Yes.

Q At that time were there or were there not tears in your eyes and were you not crying?
Mr. Harding: Objection, the question is compound.

By Mr. Merce:

Q Were you crying when you went to see Mr. Kimes to talk to him about the way that Mrs. Kimes was treating you?
Mr. Harding: Objection, leading.
Mr. Cobeaga: I'm also going to object because I think it's a misstatement of the earlier testimony of the witness.
I believe she didn't say she went to Mr. Kimes, rather it was Mr. Kimes that came to her.

By Mr. Merce:
Q Adela, after you had been—had the wooden

coat hangers broken over your body and after you had been repeatedly struck with the wire coat hangers on the back of your legs, what did you do next?
A There, I stayed in the room.

Q *Who was the next person that you saw?*
A The gentleman [Ken Kimes].

Q *Did he come to you or did you go to him?*
A He went.

Q *Are you saying he came into the room where you were?*
A Yes.

Q *What were you doing at the time he came into the room?*
  I was crying.

Q *How long was this after you had been beaten with the wooden and wire coat hangers?*
A Afterwards.

Q *Can you estimate how long afterwards?*
A Like ten minutes.

Q *What if anything did Mr. Kimes say to you?*
A He told me why I was crying.

Q *Did he ask you why you were crying?*
A Yes.

Q *How did you respond?*

A I told him because the lady had beaten me.

*Q And then what did Mr. Kimes say if
anything?*
A He said that he didn't understand.

Q Did he say anything else?
A No.

*Q Were you wearing shorts at the time that
Mrs. Kimes beat you with the wooden and wire
coat hangers?*
  Mr. Cobeaga: Objection, leading.

  By Mr. Merce:
Q Or were you wearing long pants?
  Mr. Cobeaga: Objection, leading.

  By Mr. Merce:
*Q Would you just tell us what clothes you had
on if any at the time that Mrs. Kimes beat you
with the wooden and wire coat hangers?*
A I had shorts and like a top.

*Q Do you know whether, at the time that Mr.
Kimes came into the room after the beating, if
there were any marks on your body that had
been left by the coat hangers?*
A Yes.

Q Were there marks?
A Yes.

Q Do you know what they looked like?

A Like lines.

Q Where were the lines?
A On my legs.

*Q Did you say anything else to Mr. Kimes after
he said he didn't understand?*
*A I told him I wanted to go back to Costa
Mesa.*

*Q What if anything did he say after you told
him that you wanted to go back to Costa Mesa?*
*A Later he said that he didn't understand
because everything there was all right.*

*Q Did he say that later after—could you
explain what you mean by the word later?*
A After a few minutes.

*Q Was there anything else said beween you and
Mr. Kimes at that point?*
*A I told him that nothing was all right because
I didn't know anything about my family.*

Q And what did he say to you if anything?
A Later the lady arrived and he left.

Q Did he ask you why you were crying?
      Mr. Harding: Objection, leading.
      The Witness: Yes.

      By Mr. Merce:
Q What did you say to him about that?
A Because the lady has hit me.

Q How did he respond if he did respond?
A He only said that he didn't understand.

Q Did he speak Spanish?
A Yes.

Q After that beating with the wooden and wire coat hangers, why didn't you leave the house that you were being kept in Hawaii?
A Because I was afraid.

Q During the time that you stayed in Hawaii, did you or did you not feel that you were free to leave when you wanted?
A I don't understand your question.

Q During the time that you were staying in Hawaii with the Kimes, did you feel free to leave their house?
A Yes.

Q Why didn't you leave then?
A Because I thought that the lady would reach me or get me.

Q What did you think would happen to you if she did reach you or get you?
A That she was going beat me again.

Q Did that feeling at all make you feel that you were not free to leave the house?
    Mr. Harding: I would object to the question, it's been asked and answered by the witness.

Mr. Cobeaga: And is leading.

Mr. Merce: Let me rephrase it.

By Mr. Merce:

Q Did you feel you were free to leave the house or did you feel you were being kept as a prisoner in the house?

Mr. Cobeaga: Objection, asked and answered and leading.

Mr. Harding: I join in the same objection, also it's a compound question.

The Interpreter: I didn't translate your question.

Mr. Merce: Let me rephrase the question.

By Mr. Merce:

Q Did you feel at any time while you were in Hawaii that you were a prisoner at the house where you were kept?

Mr. Cobeaga: Objection, leading and effectively asked and answered before.

(A recess is called)

Q You said that Mrs. Kimes burned you.
A Yes.

Q How did she burn you?
A She would throw hot water at me on my back.

Q She did that in Miami, didn't she?
A Yes.

Q That was the only time she did it, wasn't it?
A Yes.

Q Tell me how that happened.
A How that happened or why she burned me?

*Q Start with why she burned you. Why did she
throw the hot water on your back.*
*A Because at the hotel we had a little stove,
electric stove, and I burnt a hamburger. That's
why she burnt me.*

Q Were you cooking at the hotel?
A Yes. We would warm up water for coffee.

Q So you burned a hamburger?
A I didn't burn it. It got burnt.

Q It got burnt.
A Yes. It got burnt.

Q She threw hot water on your back?
A Yes.

*Q Where were you standing when she put the
hot water on your back?*
*A She took my clothes out, and she put me in
the bathroom.*

> *Interpreter Munoz: "She threw me in the
shower."*
> *The Witness: She took me in the bathroom.
She removed my clothes and threw me—*
> *Mr. Cobeaga: We'll start all over.*

Interpreter Hess: The thing is, if I may, I understand it one way, and she understands it a different way. But she knows the witness. Maybe she's using that particular way in another sense than the one I use. That's all. So I don't know.

Mr. Cobeaga: I understand.

By Mr. Cobeaga:

Q If you could, explain again what Mrs. Kimes did after the hamburger got burned.
A It got burnt, and she called me stupid, and she forced me to take my clothes away. And then she made me go into the bathtub.

Q Then what happened after you got to the bathtub?
A She locked me in, and then she warm up water in the little stove. And she opened the door, and she would throw it at me.

Q Were you taking a shower at the time?
A No.

Q Were you taking a bath when she did this?
A No, nothing.

Q You were just standing there?
A I was standing there.

Q She threw hot water from the stove on your back?
A Yes.

Q How many times did she throw hot water?

A Like five times.

Q Why was she doing it? Why did she want to put hot water on you?
  Because I—because the hamburger got burnt.

Q Did she want you to be washing with the water?
A No. No.

Q Was this punishment?
  Yes.

Q The water, you said it burned you.
A Yes. Because I didn't have any marks, but she would throw it, and my back was like itching.

> *Interpreter Munoz: Stinging?*
> *The Witness: Sting.*

> *By Mr. Cobeaga:*
Q Did you cry?
A Yes.

Q After she quit throwing the water on you, what did you do?
A I left the bathroom and I put my clothes on.

Q Then what did you do?
A I stayed there in the room.

Q Did you tell Teresa [a tutor] what happened?
A Yes.

Q What did Teresa say?

A That she was sorry.

Q Did you say anything to Mrs. Kimes? Did you say "Don't do that" or "Don't do that again," something like that?
A Yes, I told her.

(A noon recess is called)

Q Miss Sanchez, you've told us this morning that Mrs. Kimes slapped you, hit you with hangers, and hit you with a belt. Is that correct?
A Yes.

Q. And she hit you with the belt that one time. Is that true?
A Yes.

Q And when she did hit you, there was never any blood, was there?
A No.

Q And you never saw a doctor, did you?
A When?

Q After she hit you.
A No.

Q How long were the Kimes gone from the house in Hawaii in December of 1984 before you left?

A A few weeks.

Q And who was at the house with you after the Kimeses left?
A A lady.

Q Was her name Bessie [Ken Kimes' aunt, Elizabeth Wardshaw]?
A Yes.

Q And what did Bessie do?
A She would stay there and she would be following me.

Q What was her job?
A She would just be there in the house with me.

EXHIBITS

EXHIBIT A

Were They Wed?

Marriage Certificate

BOOK 622   No. B 313124

State of Nevada } ss.
County of Clark,

This is to Certify that the undersigned Rev Albert Alalouf did on the 5TH day of APRIL A.D. 19 81 at World Famous Chapel of the Bells LAS VEGAS Nevada join in lawful Wedlock KENNETH K. KIMES of HONOLULU State of HAWAII and SANTE SINGHRS of HONOLULU State of HAWAII with their mutual consent, in the presence of MicHAEL S RoJo who was a witness.

Calvary Grace Church

TO BE GIVEN TO THE RECORDER

Kimes family members say this marriage certificate announcing a wedding at the "World Famous Chapel of The Bells" in Las Vegas may be a phony. Las Vegas officials say it may or may not be real. The belief that it's a fake is based on Ken's repeated statements to family members that he and Sante never married. The date of marriage above is six years after Kenny's birth.

EXHIBIT B

An Erroneous Death Deed

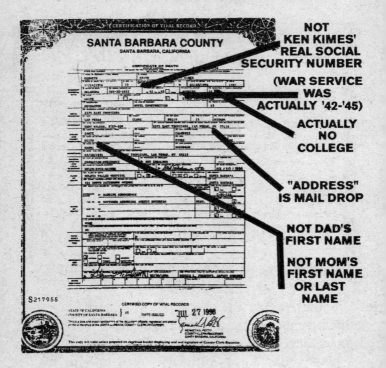

NOT KEN KIMES' REAL SOCIAL SECURITY NUMBER

(WAR SERVICE WAS ACTUALLY '42-'45)

ACTUALLY NO COLLEGE

"ADDRESS" IS MAIL DROP

NOT DAD'S FIRST NAME

NOT MOM'S FIRST NAME OR LAST NAME

EXHIBIT C
Forgery 101?

When Kenny Kimes signed this lease for a University of California at Santa Barbara group house on February 16, 1995, he signed with this dramatic flourish.

To the best of my knowledge these are some of the events as they occurred.

DATED this _10TH_ day of November, 1995.

Ken Kimes
KEN KIMES

But, when Kenny Kimes signed this response before a notary public nine months later in response to Carrie Louise Grammer's request for a restraining order seeking protection from his violent behavior, his signature seemed much subdued.

EXHIBIT D
Sante's Pun Fun?

On the afternoon of January 8, 1996, we contacted Mr Kono in order to get an explanation of why Mr Kimes was being arraigned on the November 16, 1995 complaint. He expressed surprise that the hearing had not resolved the complaint filed by his client. Mr Kono's explanation was that the sheriff's report (#95-19848) was inadvertently not incorporated in the order signed by yourself on November 17, 1995. After appraising Mr Kono of the circumstances, he said he would take care of the matter with Deputy District Attorney McIntosh. At this point, we have not been contacted by Mr Kono as to the outcome of his discussion with Mr McIntosh and if the matter has been corrected.

As you might well imagine, this recent turn of events has been greatly unfair and disturbing to us, particularly when we thought the hearing and your ruling on November 17, 1995 had resolved this matter. It is for this reason that we are asking for your assistance to resolve this matter before the court date of January 16, 1996. I have rushed here from the Bahamas to try to clear up this matter.

My son and his roommates have been the victims of harassment by Ms Grammer for months, which has adversely affected their studies and interfered with the quiet enjoyment of their otherwise peaceful home.

We are advised that communication from you will finally resolve this unfortunate matter and not consume any more of the court's time regarding matters of a cat soiling a bedspread and untrue allegations of a phone call.

Words cannot express our gratitude for your consideration at this time.

Respectfully Yours,

Santé Khan

Who says grifters don't have a sense of humor? Sante Kimes sent a letter to a California judge on January 9, 1996, signing her name as Santé Khan (pronounced *con*).

EXHIBIT E

A Typical Sante Kimes Stalking Horse Has Second Thoughts

<u>AFFIDAVIT OF BEVERLY R. BATES</u>

STATE OF HAWAII   )
) ss.
CITY AND COUNTY OF HONOLULU   )

       BEVERLY BATES, being first duly sworn upon oath, deposes and says that:

       1.   My name is Beverly R. Bates. I reside in Honolulu, Hawaii. I have personal knowledge of the matters contained herein and am competent to testify to the same.

       2.   I have been acquainted with Santee and Kenneth Kimes since approximately 1974. We were neighbors on Portlock Road.

       3.   In 1977 or 1978, Mrs. Kimes called me on the telephone and said she was being sued by a contractor who was attempting to serve her with legal documents. She appeared to be very upset with the fact that she had received the documents and was crying. She asked me if I would go to see her lawyer and tell him that it was I who had been served with the legal documents and not her. At first, I strenuously objected but she implored me to help her out and reluctantly, I agreed. She told me that if I didn't help her, she would lose her house. The instructions Mrs. Kimes gave me were to dress up like her and go to her lawyer's office. He would then meet me and take me to see the sheriff who had served the legal documents at the

Kimes' residence. I was to tell the sheriff that I was the person who had been served rather than Mrs. Kimes. In fact, Mrs. Kimes told me that it was she who had been served with these documents.

4.   Mrs. Kimes then said that I would have to look like her in order to persuade the sheriff that it was I rather than she who had been served. Mrs. Kimes nearly always wears white dresses or muu muus and black wigs. She also wears heavy eye lashes and make up. She met me at my office and brought white clothing, make up, a wig, and eye lashes with her. I dressed up in her clothes, wore one of her wigs, and she made up my face with her eye lashes and make up.

5.   I then went to her lawyer's office and introduced myself. He thanked me for coming, and I accompanied him to the Office of the Sheriff.

6.   As soon as the Sheriff saw me, he told me that I was not the one that he had actually served and that he had served someone else. As soon as he confronted me, I realized that I could not go through with what Mrs. Kimes was asking me to do, and I acknowledged to Mrs. Kimes' attorney that I had not actually been served and that it was Mrs. Kimes who had received the legal documents. We then left the Sheriff's office. I understand that the lawyer then withdrew from representing the Kimes.

7.   After I got back to my office, Kenneth Kimes called me and thanked me for trying to help them.

FURTHER AFFIANT SAYETH NAUGHT.

Beverly R. Bates
BEVERLY R. BATES

Subscribed and sworn to before me
this 29th day of _June_, 1987.

Georgiana B. Palanlag
Notary Public, State of Hawaii

My Commission Expires: 4-4-88

Notes on Sources and Acknowledgments

More than 100 people were interviewed for this book. Most spoke forthrightly and on the record but, not surprisingly, many asked for anonymity, citing a fear of retribution from Sante Kimes. When the author pointed out that she was being held in jail without bail, several sources expressed the belief that it would only be a matter of time before she and Kenny would be free.

To produce a book as complete as this, the author relied on a nationwide network that provided invaluable assistance. In Orange County, California, there was Lusa Hung, Barbara J. Palermo, and Linda Nakama Contreras; in Los Angeles, Roberta Ostroff, Steve McArthur, and Larry Haile; in Santa Barbara, Ken Tsoi and Alisa Frye; in San Francisco, Steve Weiss; in San Diego, Gustav J. Bujkovsky, Esq., Karen Di Donna, and Kanye "the Apache" Dunbar; and, in Sacramento, Jim Abrams. In Nevada, there was Alan Shadrake and the Raho family in Las Vegas; in Carson City, Duane Glanzman and Major Cindy Kirkland; and in Reno, Ruth Tanis.

Also Jim Blackner in Cedar City, Utah; Charles F. Catterlin in Harlingen, Texas; Stuart Ho and the offices of David C. Schutter, Esquire in Honolulu; and Bob Calvert; Pat Gregor, Tom Kuncl, and Joe Mullins in southern Florida; Charlsanne Atkins covered the Bahamas.

In Washington, Eric J. Davis of the National Cathedral taught me the difference between a gargoyle and a grotesque; in New Jersey, Kelli Richman set me straight on the topography of its swamplands; and in New York, Miki Ben-Kiki, Lisa Arcella, Richard Gooding, Janice Herbert, Diane Jaust, Dina Andrew, Larry Celona, Diane Santiago, Mitch Newsom, Tracy Connor, and Steve Marsh, all helped get this project started, as did the New York newspapers and those local TV news crews who covered the disappearance of Irene Silverman like a thick blanket.

I'd also like to recognize the employees of the following institutions who helped me find documents: The Lincoln Center Library for the Performing Arts; the Library of Congress; and the library of the American Hotel and Motel Association.

The idea for this book came from Miriam Goderich of the Jane Dystel Literary Agency. Charlie Spicer, who knows more about crime than Al Capone and John Gotti combined, was the only editor who could have handled a project like this.

As always, my wife, Georgiana, was there to research, edit, and critique, as was Brenda Atkins, who pored over the manuscript with a sharp pencil.

To all these great people, both new and old friends, thank you.

"AN INVALUABLE BOOK FOR ANYONE WHO WANTS TO UNDERSTAND SERIAL MURDER."

—Joseph Wambaugh

WHOEVER FIGHTS MONSTERS

My Twenty Years Tracking Serial Killers for the FBI

ROBERT K. RESSLER & TOM SHACHTMAN

He coined the phrase "serial killer", he advised Thomas Harris on *The Silence of the Lambs*, he has gone where no else has dared to go: inside the minds of the 20th century's most prolific serial killers. From Charles Manson to Edmund Kemper, follow former FBI agent Robert K. Ressler's ingenious trail from the scene of the crime to the brain of a killer in this fascinating true crime classic.

"THE REAL THING. ABSOLUTELY MESMERIZING."

—Ann Rule, author of *Small Sacrifices*

**AVAILABLE WHEREVER BOOKS ARE SOLD
FROM ST. MARTIN'S PAPERBACKS**

For six terror-filled years, he couldn't be stopped—
until one journalist ingeniously cracked his twisted code...

SLEEP MY LITTLE DEAD

The True Story of the
Zodiac Killer

Kieran Crowley

The award-winning *New York Post* reporter whose
brilliant work helped crack the Zodiac Killer's
secret code reveals the inside story—as only he can
tell it—of the man who terrorized the streets of
New York City for six years, stalking, savagely
attacking, and often killing his unsuspecting victims in cold blood.

**AVAILABLE WHEREVER BOOKS ARE SOLD
FROM ST. MARTIN'S PAPERBACKS**